THE JOHANNINE CIRCLE

THE
JOHANNINE CIRCLE

by

Oscar Cullmann

Translated by John Bowden

THE WESTMINSTER PRESS

Philadelphia

Translated from the German
*Der johanneische Kreis, Sein Platz im Spätjudentum,
in der Jüngerschaft Jesu und im Urchristentum,*
published 1975 by J. C. B. Mohr (Paul Siebeck), Tübingen

© Oscar Cullmann 1975

Translation © SCM Press Ltd. 1976

Published by The Westminster Press
Philadelphia, Pennsylvania

PRINTED IN THE UNITED STATES OF AMERICA

Library of Congress Cataloging in Publication Data

Cullmann, Oscar.
    The Johannine circle.

    Translation of Der johanneische Kreis.
    Bibliography: p.
    Includes index.
    1. Johannine school. 2. Bible. N.T. John—
Criticism, interpretation, etc. I. Title.
BS2615.2.C8413   296.3   75-42249
    ISBN 0-664-20744-8

*To the Protestant Faculty of Theology
in the Ludwig-Maximilians-Universität, Munich,
with gratitude for my semester as their guest in the summer of 1974,
and in memory of my revered colleague
Leonhard Goppelt*

CONTENTS

PREFACE

FOR MANY YEARS I have been occupied with the Gospel of John and have given a number of lectures on it in my work in Basle and in Paris. I have taught and at the same time learnt from the ever-growing literature on the subject. This has increasingly compelled me to consider the circumstances of the origin of the Gospel, and here for the first time I present a synthesis of the numerous articles which I have devoted to the subject. At first I thought of this book as the introduction to a commentary which I intend to write. But it has grown too long, and as I have to go into questions which exceed the usual limits of 'Introduction', I prefer to offer it as an independent investigation. However, exegetical work has led to my views, and they should be examined and confirmed by a legitimate circular process which involves exegesis.

The best context for solving the various problems posed by the Gospel seems to me to be that of an investigation into the origin, character and setting of the 'Johannine circle', which stands behind the Gospel and continues its theological concern. The existence of this circle can hardly be challenged, even if the individual personality of the author has a more distinct literary and theological profile than that of the other evangelists.

I must ask the reader not to take offence if I quote my own articles on the Fourth Gospel in addition to the work of many other authors. As my own articles are all concerned with the synthesis which I attempt here, and provide the foundation for it, I must refer to them often, since I can only summarize their findings in the present context.

Forty-five years ago I wrote a book on the Pseudo-Clementine writings and the relationship between gnosticism and Jewish Christianity. It was my first book, and may already be regarded as preparatory work towards establishing the origin of the Johannine

circle. I have never abandoned the argument which I presented
there, that the earliest Christianity is rooted in a marginal form of
Palestinian Judaism, and it has guided all my work on the milieu
and the spiritual home of the Gospel of John in a particular direction.
At that time, despite the valuable insights of Old and New Testament scholars and those engaged in the history of religions, we did
not know more or less heterodox Judaism as well as we do now, after
more recent discoveries of manuscripts. Meanwhile, such Judaism
has been brought much closer to us by the evaluation of those manuscripts, in work which has also been connected with the Gospel of
John.

I have always been concerned not only to establish the origin of
the Johannine circle within Judaism but also to define its position
within primitive Christianity. Judaism in the time of Jesus cannot be
accommodated within the framework of an earlier pattern which
saw no Hellenistic Judaism in Palestine and Hellenistic Judaism in
the Diaspora; similarly, we cannot follow the Tübingen school in
dividing earliest Christianity into Palestinian Jewish Christianity and
Hellenistic Gentile Christianity.

In the annual of the École des Hautes-Études in Paris for 1953/54,
a work of mine was published on the Hellenist mission in Samaria in
John 4 and Acts 8; in 1958 I presented to a conference of the Society
for New Testament Studies (SNTS) my theory of the triangular relationship between the Gospel of John, the group around Stephen,
and Samaria and heterodox Judaism, with special stress on the liturgical connections between them. I was very pleasantly surprised
when this theory was confirmed indirectly from a different perspective, and in quite a different way, through a comparison of New
Testament and Samaritan texts by English-speaking specialists in
Samaritan studies. At the same time, these scholars provided the
solid foundations which were needed. So my argument may now
find a wider hearing than before, even outside the English-speaking
world, especially since, as I shall try to show, it can be related to
earlier works by other scholars on gnostic influences on Judaism.

Investigations into the spiritual home of the Gospel of John and
its suggested place in earliest Christianity have still to be applied to
the solution of the *other* problems which the Gospel raises. The
attempt which I have made here to throw a new light on these other

problems has produced results which differ both from the tradition of the church and from the views now put forward by the majority of scholars, even if they can be supported by the testimony of the Gospel. I would therefore beg the supporters of both points of view not to label my conclusions in their customary way. The fact that my work is independent of *both* points of view should put them on their guard.

I have been extremely careful about constructing hypotheses and have restrained myself as far as possible, but every now and then I have had to make conjectures which must be no more than hypotheses, however confident I may be about their probability. I must, however, stress that it is impossible to avoid hypotheses entirely in attempting to solve what is called the Johannine riddle; hypotheses are inevitable throughout Johannine scholarship, *even where* a majority *'consensus'* seems to have been reached. I would certainly not underestimate the value of an academic consensus in the investigation of New Testament problems – my own investigation demonstrates this in a number of places –, nor would I underestimate the agreed view of the church, which we call 'tradition'. But neither of these can keep scholars from trying out new approaches, when they seem to be necessary.

In addition, I hope that the arguments advanced here, above all those relating to the *purpose* of the evangelist, will help to further the interpretation of his work, which sees with profound theological insight the earthly life of Jesus as the climax and the consummation of the divine revelation to men and sets out to communicate this insight. Consequently, what I have written is meant to be not only 'Introduction' in the technical sense; it is also meant to be a prelude to exegesis.

Munich, Summer 1974

I must thank all those who helped me with the preparation of the manuscript and its printing, in Munich and in Basle: above all my sister and Ulrich Wilhelm, who also made the index.

Basle, January 1975

ABBREVIATIONS

BA	*Biblical Archaeologist*, New Haven
BJRL	*Bulletin of the John Rylands Library*, Manchester
BZAW	Beihefte zur *Zeitschrift für die alttestamentliche Wissenschaft*, Berlin
CBQ	*Catholic Biblical Quarterly*, Washington DC
EB	Echter Bibel, Würzburg
EvTh	*Evangelische Theologie*, Münich
ExpT	*Expository Times*, Edinburgh
HNT	Handbuch zum Neuen Testament, Tübingen
HTR	*Harvard Theological Review*, Cambridge, Mass.
ICC	International Critical Commentary, Edinburgh
JBL	*Journal of Biblical Literature*, Philadelphia
NCB	New Century Bible, London
NT	*Novum Testamentum*, Leiden
NTD	Das Neue Testament Deutsch, Göttingen
NTS	*New Testament Studies*, Cambridge
OrLov	*Orientalia et Biblica Lovaniensia*, Louvain
RB	*Revue Biblique*, Paris
RSR	*Revue des Sciences Religieuses*, Strasbourg
SBT	Studies in Biblical Theology, London
TBC	Torch Bible Commentaries, London
TDNT	G. Kittel - G. Friedrich (eds.), *Theological Dictionary of the New Testament*, Grand Rapids, Michigan
TR	*Theologische Rundschau*, Tübingen
TZ	*Theologische Zeitschrift*, Basle
VigC	*Vigiliae Christianae*, Amsterdam
ZNW	*Zeitschrift für die neutestamentliche Wissenschaft*, Berlin
ZTK	*Zeitschrift für Theologie und Kirche*, Tübingen

If we seek to identify a 'Johannine circle' within early Christianity we must begin with the literary and theological characteristics of our chief source, the Gospel of John. The first four chapters are therefore devoted to this question.

I

THE LITERARY UNITY, SOURCES AND REDACTION OF THE GOSPEL OF JOHN

As soon as we try to describe the special features of the Fourth Gospel, we come up against a greater difficulty than those found in the study of the synoptic gospels. Books about what is now called redaction criticism are able to give us a more or less exact picture of the literary and theological characteristics of the authors of the Gospels of Mark, Matthew and Luke. But the Gospel of John has been stripped down to reveal a number of sources, each with its own different peculiarities; indeed, the whole work has been dissected into a series of successive editions and redactions, each assigned to a particular author or a particular trend. In some theories one such redaction may even be diametrically opposed to the one which went before. In these last instances, it would be particularly tricky to use the Gospel to give definition to a 'Johannine circle'.

True, scholars concerned with the synoptic gospels also speak of sources when discussing the synoptic problem or pursuing form-critical investigations. But in more recent scholarship the literary unity of the Gospel of John has been shattered in quite a different way. Anyone reading my attempt to describe the Johannine way of presenting the life of Jesus and the theology which underlies it might therefore be tempted to ask, 'But on which of these hypothetical documents are you basing your case?', thus putting the whole enterprise in question. We must therefore begin by considering the scope of the problem.

Inconsistencies within the Gospel have long been noted: verses, or even whole chapters which do not follow easily from one another; peculiarities of style or vocabulary in particular sections; variations in theological concepts or approaches. Historical evaluations also differ: some of the details of the Gospel seem to derive from very old traditions, at times even better historically than those in the synoptics, whereas others represent a more advanced stage of development.

Three explanations of this situation have been proposed:

1. The work as we have it is the end-result of a variety of successive editions or redactions.

2. Sources have been incorporated into the Gospel with a greater or lesser degree of success.

3. In a number of places, pages have become disordered, but it is possible to recognize the original order and remove all difficulties.

These three types of explanation are usually combined.

Julius Wellhausen, the doyen of Old Testament study, did a great deal to direct study of the Gospel of John in this direction by applying the methods of Old Testament source criticism, *mutatis mutandis*, to John.[1] He was followed by E. Schwartz,[2] and Rudolf Bultmann's commentary went furthest along the same path.

We must now look more closely at the three types of solution.

1.   *Multiple redactions*

The last verses of ch. 21 themselves suggest that one or more disciples of the author published the Gospel after his death, and are therefore already an indication of the existence of a Johannine 'circle'. Whoever is speaking here is not, in fact, the author of the rest of the Gospel. He offers an explanation: 'This is the disciple who is bearing witness to these things, and who has written these things; and *we* know that *his* testimony is true' (21.24). As the last verse of the preceding chapter (20.31) is clearly the conclusion to the whole work, it is very probable that the whole of ch. 21 has been added by this same redactor – or perhaps there were more than one. That does not rule out the possibility that he put down in writing the narrative of the appearance of Christ by the Sea of Tiberias recorded in this chapter, or composed it from oral reminiscences of his master, the author of the Gospel.

All this suggests that the same redactor (or redactors) may not have been content with adding a postscript; at the same time he (or they) may have rearranged the whole work, chs. 1–20. Consequently, almost all modern commentators reckon with the possibility of at least *one* final redaction of the *entire* Gospel. It may even have been that the author died before completing the work, leaving the final redactor(s) to finish it.[3] This would be one explanation of most of the unevennesses which can be found in chs. 1–20.

Some of them are particularly striking. A favourite example in this context is that of the farewell discourses in chs. 14–17. At the end of ch. 14, in v. 31, we read: 'Rise, let us go hence.' Surprisingly enough, however, the disciples do not rise after these words; Jesus continues: 'I am the true vine,' and then three long chapters follow. The narrative is only taken up again at the end of the farewell discourses, in 18.1, with the words: 'When Jesus had spoken these words, he went forth with his disciples across the Kidron valley, where there was a garden.' This verse can easily be understood as a direct continuation of the invitation in 14.31. In that case, everything in between, chs. 15–17, would have been inserted later. Was this insertion made by the author himself or by the redactor whose voice we hear in 21.24ff.?[4]

Many exegetes assume that the whole Gospel underwent more than one redaction and assign to each redaction a particular literary or theological aim. The different hypotheses have numerous variants. Some assign the redactions to different authors, while others (especially W. Wilkens,[5] and to some degree also R. E. Brown)[6] think that the evangelist himself reshaped his work several times before the last editor made his final revision.

Once we have to reckon with the possibility of one revision or even more, the way is open for a variety of attempts to dissect the Gospel. R. E. Brown[7] and R. Schnackenburg[8] provide a good survey of the countless solutions (which have continued to increase in number since),[9] but the most striking thing about them is their dissimilarity. The need to proceed with some restraint in this area is thus all the more evident. While the confusing divergencies between the various hypotheses should not prevent us from considering theories of redactional activity in the exegesis of some Johannine passages, these divergencies are so wide that considerable caution is necessary. Schnackenburg takes great pains over this in his commentary, as is particularly evident when we compare it, say, with that of Bultmann, who attributes a quite radical revision to an 'ecclesiastical' redactor, a revision which is said to run directly counter to the purpose of the original Gospel, written against a gnostic background (e.g. by introducing sacramentalism and a futurist eschatology). In a different way, R. E. Brown believes that he can distinguish a number of redactions with a considerable degree of precision.

Critical examination of all attempts at dissection of this kind should also take into account the fact that modern logic and modes of thought are not necessarily the same as those of an early Christian thinker.[10] Instead of building one idea upon another, the early Christian would rather consider the same truth from different perspectives, with the result that some sections appear to be either intolerable repetitions or irreconcilable contradictions which would not give this impression to a redactor or even to an original author.

In particular, if an attempt to distinguish different redactions or different sources (a topic which will be discussed later) goes too far, it comes up against a barrier. For it is beyond question that a degree of unity can be followed right through the Gospel: unity of language, unity of style and indeed unity of theological purpose.

Eduard Schweizer[11] and E. Ruckstuhl[12] have sought to demonstrate a unitary style, in particular as a counter to Bultmann's arguments. Their conclusions should be taken into account when assessing all other divisions. It also seems to me to be equally important that a single *purpose* can be demonstrated, not just as it has been imposed through the final revision of the work, but also as a constant feature, so to speak, of all its parts. What I shall have to say in the next chapter about the evangelist's purpose therefore seems to me to be of special significance. And if we can detect a strong personality behind this purpose, whole presence can be felt everywhere, we should at least hesitate before attributing the conception of such a purpose to a mere redactor. Even where we find evidence of a redactor, we must ask whether he might not have been under the influence of this strong personality: individual instances apart, the redactor's own personal contribution should not be exaggerated. For this reason, as has already been noted, some scholars, while often supporting theories which presuppose quite wide-scale divisions into different redactions, think in terms of redactions made by the author *himself*. Such a view is particularly often held in connection with ch. 21.

Now I am not concerned to rule out altogether different redactions made by later hands; I do, however, wish to impose some restraint on sweeping proposals which are devoid of any self-criticism. It is not so easy to distinguish redactions that we can take them as the *starting point* for all discussions about exegesis or the determination of the origin and authorship of the Gospel.[13] More recent attempts to make neat distinctions between a variety of versions often prompt the question which author of which putative redaction deserves the title 'evangelist'. In these attempts a decision often seems quite arbitrary.

Nevertheless, we may keep in mind the factor which is important for the hypothesis of a 'Johannine circle': the author had disciples who appear as redactors in the production and revision of the Gospel. It can also be demonstrated that even before, and during, the composition of his book he could rely on a group of like-minded people and perhaps even on their written contributions. This brings us to the question of sources.

2. Sources

What was said about redactors can also be applied to the question of sources. If every part of the Gospel is stamped by a unitary purpose which betrays a strong personality to such a degree that the style, too, is affected, can we suppose that whole sources were taken over more or less unexamined? Might we not have to presuppose a very personal use of such sources by the original author? Even further aspects should be taken into account.

As the Gospel of John has a number of features in common with the *synoptic* gospels, and especially with Luke, the first question is whether the author knew them or at least made use of one or other of them. To begin with, however, it must be stressed that nowhere, not even in the passion narrative, is the literary affinity so close that a *literary* relationship *has to* be supposed comparable to that which exists between the individual synoptic gospels themselves. Some

assertions have, of course, been made: first, that the evangelist presupposes a knowledge of the synoptic gospels when, for example, in
1.40 he introduces Andrew as the brother of Peter before Peter has
even been mentioned; secondly, that in other passages he seems
deliberately to correct information in the synoptic gospels, as for
example in 3.24, according to which at a certain point John the
Baptist had not yet been put into prison. But in each case it is suffi-
cient to assume that the author knew the *tradition* underlying the
synoptic gospels, without necessary referring to the *documents* themselves.[14]

By and large, however, the Johannine account of the life of Jesus
is quite different from that of the synoptic gospels, in both geographical context (a number of journeys to Jerusalem instead of just
one, a number of stays in Judaea instead of just one) and chronological framework (the public activity of Jesus lasts two or three
years according to the passovers mentioned, instead of just one). The
difference from the synoptic gospels is so great here, and on the
whole so little stress is laid on it, that in the parallel passages there is
an increasing inclination to suppose that the Gospel of John and the
written synoptic gospels each made *independent* use of a common
tradition.[15]

In addition to the synoptic gospels and the synoptic tradition,
special Johannine sources are also considered, and attempts are often
made to identify them. Bultmann, in particular, set himself to this
task and achieved noteworthy results. Following the work of predecessors,[16] he noted in particular that in 2.11 and 4.54 miracles *are
numbered*; this led him to distinguish a source containing seven *semeia*
(miracle stories) and also a source of *discourses* with a gnostic character, dealing with revelation. These would both have been linked with
the passion narrative. Recently, R. T. Fortna has even attempted to
reconstruct the *semeia* source verse by verse in the form of a gospel
like the synoptics but independent of them;[17] it would not be very
old, and after an introduction about the testimony of John the
Baptist and the call of the first disciples would have narrated the
miracles of Jesus and his passion, without giving his teaching. Before
Fortna, H. Becker made an attempt to define more closely the other
source posited by Bultmann, containing the revelation discourses.[18]

At this point we should also take into account the unity of style, language and purpose which we noted in considering analyses in terms of different redactions.[19] While this does not exclude the possibility that the author of the Gospel used written sources, it does make problematical all attempts to *identify* their extent, despite Fortna's efforts in methodology and his attempts to contrast his statistics with those of Ruckstuhl. In criticizing Bultmann's division into sources, C. H. Dodd already pointed to the close link between the miracles and the discourses.[20]

I would prefer to speak of special Johannine *traditions* rather than of Johannine sources. The author will have known on the one hand a tradition *common* to *all* branches of early Christianity and made familiar to us through the synoptic gospels, and on the other a *separate tradition*, of special interest to us, which came down to him in the *particular circle* to which he belonged. B. Noack has called attention to the oral Johannine tradition,[21] but we may at least reckon with the possibility that *in part* it may have already been given fixed form in writing.

This tradition had probably undergone some development by the time that the Gospel of John was composed. We may therefore think in principle of sketching out a history of Johannine tradition along the same lines as the form-critical work undertaken by Bultmann on the synoptic tradition.[22]

In the following chapters we shall have occasion to speak of at least an important and *distinct group*, if not a particular *school*, within the Christianity of the first century, representing a different type from that of the synoptics. Certain traditions about the life and teaching of Jesus must have been alive in this group, and like any oral tradition they must have undergone some development. However, the situation differs from that in the synoptic tradition in that the author of the Fourth Gospel is more than a mere collector, more than a spokesman for a tradition handed down through this community. He was not content to reproduce these traditions according to certain individual points of view which can be investigated by means of 'redaction criticism'. On the contrary, he must have been a very strong literary and theological personality in quite a different way, which we have still to establish, not to be compared with any of the other evangelists.

He is aware on the one hand of having special historical traditions at his disposal, and on the other – if I am right in supposing that at least the content of the farewell discourses (chs. 14–17) comes from him – of being inspired by the 'spirit of truth' to reveal the deeper meaning and significance of these facts, so that he can deal with the speeches of Jesus in a sovereign manner. This awareness, to which we shall be returning frequently, gives him an *authority* unlike that to be found with any other evangelist. Even if the author has made use of written or oral traditions, he has adapted them entirely to his purpose and given them his own distinctive stamp.

The observation of a certain '*rhythm*' which characterizes some parts of the discourses, and especially the prologue, could perhaps serve as a criterion for identifying the rhythmic verses as belonging to a source and designating the prose sections which interrupt the rhythm as later additions which were made either by the evangelist or by the later redactor. Here too, however, we find ourselves on too uncertain ground to be able to use this means with too great a degree of confidence.

Our conclusion is thus analogous to that on the question of redaction: the sources lead us to posit the existence of a Johannine circle, even during the lifetime of the author. The latter, however, must have played a *predominant* part within it.

3.   *The restoration of an original order by means of the transposition of chapters and verses*

It is clear that some of the unevennesses in the present text can be corrected relatively easily by altering the present sequence of verses and even of chapters. Exegetes must examine this possibility in each individual instance. Thus even so cautious an interpreter as R. Schnackenburg suggests in his commentary that chs. 5 and 6 should be transposed. Long before him, J. H. Bernard had already made similar rearrangements. This method was taken to very great lengths by R. Bultmann. However, although it is legitimate in principle for the construction of a hypothesis, its use calls for some degree of restraint. For as we have already noted, on the one hand what we may regard as a logical order may not necessarily correspond to the thought and practice of the author. On the other hand, we have to explain how what is supposed to be the present disorder,

attested moreover by all the manuscripts, could come about if everything had earlier been in logical order.[23] No theological reasons can
usually be found. Should we follow J. H. Bernard and others in
thinking of an accident, of pages becoming mixed up? It should
first be noted that it would be more difficult to disarrange the pages
once a scroll had been made. But even if we are to think of unbound
leaves, we should not forget that these usually end in the middle of a
sentence, which is continued on the following sheet, so that any dis-
arrangement would be easy to notice. If the present order or disorder is not original, we shall have to attribute it to clumsy redaction,
though this explanation also has its problems.

4. Conclusions

All exegetes must exercise some restraint in their discipline; this is
also true in an investigation of the origin of the Gospel or an attempt
to establish the characteristics of the Johannine circle by considering
the literary problems of redaction, sources and possible transposi-
tions outlined here. It may well be thought necessary to consider the
hypothesis of interference by a final redactor or a group of final
redactors or even intermediary redactors when interpreting particular passages; the hypothesis of the use of sources or an alteration in
sequence may also be kept in mind; but it must never be forgotten
that these are only hypotheses. Not only in exegesis but also in
examining the origin of the Gospel it seems to me that the unavoidable literary presuppositions should be kept as few as possible. Thus
while the new commentary by the American scholar R. E. Brown is
good in many respects, it seems to me to go too far in assuming five
stages of literary development.[24] I would suggest the following process of literary composition:[25]

1. The author, a strong personality, made use both of traditions
belonging to the common legacy of early Christianity and of a number of special traditions, either written or in oral form, coming from
the particular circles to which he belonged. We cannot rule out the
possibility that he also included personal reminiscences as well as
special traditions.

2. He was responsible for the main lines of the work as we have it
now.

3. A redactor or a group of redactors under the influence of the author and belonging to his circle revised or completed the whole work after his death.

In the following chapters, then, we shall go on to discuss the purpose of the evangelist as *such* and the other general aspects of the Gospel as *such*, although we know that it is dependent on earlier traditions and that at least one redactor, the one who added ch. 21, edited and revised the work. We must remember that even after reducing factors in this way, mistakes in identifying sources cannot be avoided. But they will not be as serious as if we take as a starting point an analysis the *precise* details of which are problematical.

This caution to be observed before we distinguish between the author of the Gospel, the redactor(s) and the sources is in no way a matter of doctrinaire conservatism. It does not arise from a misuse of critical sensibility, but on the contrary from a care for objectivity and a concern to remain within the realms of probability without too great a degree of arbitrary judgment. (Hypotheses are unavoidable and as working hypotheses can further scholarship.) Because investigations sometimes reach diametrically opposed results,[26] there seems to me to be as much risk in attributing too much to the redaction at the expense of the author as in attributing too little. Indeed, to attribute too much to redactors may be more dangerous. We must suppose that the author was capable of selecting earlier traditions and even sources and using them for his own purposes to express particular views. On the other hand, the following consideration should be borne in mind. If a view usually attributed by commentators to a later redactor did not seem to him to be *irreconcilable* with other statements in the original Gospel, is it really so much more difficult in some cases to suppose that the author of the original Gospel might have made this combination *himself*?

Finally, looking back over the problem of the Johannine circle, we may ask what distinguished the towering personality of the evangelist from the other members of his group. Quite apart from the extraordinary format of the Gospel, we should think of his intention of writing a *life of Jesus*, that is, not only creating an external, purely literary framework in a gospel to express the views of the group to which he belonged, but also showing how *the full signifi-*

cance of these views can only be recognized when they are presented in an account of the life of the incarnate Jesus. The conception of this account is his work. He shared the theological foundations for it with the whole of his circle.

It is therefore particularly important for both these questions that we should establish the purpose of the Gospel, and to that we now turn.

II

THE PURPOSE OF THE EVANGELIST

I N S E E K I N G to discover the purpose of the author in composing his life of Jesus one might be tempted to be content with his own words in 20.31: 'These things are written that you may believe that Jesus is the Christ, the Son of God, and that believing you may have life in his name.' However, this declaration is in such general terms that it is impossible to infer a more specific declaration of purpose from it. Indeed, on its basis the author has been credited with the most varied intentions. It gives no more than the general framework within which the solution should be sought.

Those commentators who believe that they can demonstrate the exact limits and theological tendencies of different editions of the Gospel try to make precise statements about the reasons why the redactor(s) changed what they had before them in any particular version. Thus Bultmann regards the evangelist as a former gnostic disciple of the sect of John the Baptist who was anxious to adapt his gnosticism to belief in Jesus Christ. The so-called 'ecclesiastical' redactor is said to have pursued a much more radical aim, namely to do away with the gnostic slant of the Gospel by introducing the church's view of the faith, which would be diametrically opposed to that of the original author. He replaced the 'futuristic eschatology' of the original Gospel by 'realized' eschatology, and the anti-sacramentalist tendency by sacramentalism. In the previous chapter we pointed out that it is difficult to make too precise a division of the Gospel into sources and different redactions. The same proviso must be made in the case of attempts to distinguish the different intentions of the various hypothetical documents supposed to make up the Gospel.

One main theme which underlies a number of attempts to define the purpose of the evangelist is the gnostic character which Rudolf Bultmann and others have detected in the Gospel. However, whereas according to Bultmann the original gnosticism of the author was considerably changed when he was converted to Christianity, Ernst Käsemann believes that even the Gospel as we have it is gnostic; indeed he goes so far as to assert that the author was bold enough to want to replace the Christianity of his time by gnosticism, through his Gospel.[1] Herbert Braun's pupil L. Schottroff takes the same line[2] (we shall have to discuss the so-called 'gnosticism' of the Gospel of John later).[3]

It is clear that the author's approach to the life of Jesus is different from that of his predecessors. He is confident in his approach, because he has special traditions about events, and is conscious of assessing all events in a particular theological perspective. Above all, he knows himself to be inspired by the Paraclete, the 'spirit of truth', to 'recall' all that Jesus said and did. We shall discuss later this 'recalling', the special mission to write a *new* life of Jesus with which the evangelist evidently believes himself to be entrusted.[4]

I would not, however, go as far as H. Windisch, who claimed that on the basis of this consciousness the author intended to replace the synoptic gospels with his own.[5] We have assumed that while he knew the synoptic tradition, he probably did not know the *written* synoptic gospels. It is, however, probably true that he is conscious of making an advance on the synoptic *tradition*. We shall be able to discuss this question in more detail when we describe the circle to which the author belonged in the chapter on his milieu. Thus it is not his purpose to displace the synoptic gospels, which he probably does not know; rather, he wishes to differ from the tradition which underlies them. His picture of Christ is not absolutely different, but is seen from another perspective. It is as though a village were now being viewed from a high mountain, when descriptions of it had hitherto been from below. With the change of viewpoint, different aspects and different details become important.

The words from 20.31 quoted above have also been taken to mean that the evangelist intended to convert unbelievers. For J. L. Martyn, polemic against the Jews is in the foreground.[6] J. A. T. Robinson and van Unnik restrict the audience to diaspora Jews.[7] A great many other explanations of the evangelist's purpose have been put forward: polemic against the Jews, polemic against heretics. Each has a grain of truth. But none seems to me to cover the central concern of the author, to which other aims are subsidiary.

The end of John 20.31 reads: 'and that believing you may have life in his name'. Thus the evangelist has the community of believers in mind. The verse can therefore be understood, as R. E. Brown, R. Schnackenburg and others suppose, to refer to a *strengthening* of the faith of those who already believe in Christ, and in fact the content of the Gospel supports such an interpretation. The mere conviction of being commissioned to write the life of Jesus in a *special* way causes the evangelist to strengthen the belief of the faithful.[8]

At this point I would like to make this 'special way' more precise by a detailed investigation of the content of the Gospel. At the same time this will help us also to be more precise about the evangelist's purpose. I shall present my argument as follows: in each individual event of the life of the *incarnate* Jesus the evangelist seeks to show that *at the same time* the *Christ present in his church* is already at work. Thus from each narrative he draws out the line leading to the risen Christ who is at work in every activity of his community: in worship, in mission, in the struggle with unbelieving Jews and heretics.

On each occasion he considers a particular *unique* event alongside its continued influence after the resurrection of Christ in *one and the same* perspective. Thus this perspective is quite different from that of Luke, who also describes the life of Christ in the community of believers apart from the life of the incarnate Jesus. Luke maintains a perspective of *chronological* sequence and therefore takes another course: the *first volume* of his work tells of the work accomplished by the 'historical' Jesus, the *second* of what he continues through his disciples. By contrast, the author of the Gospel of John seeks to consider Jesus after the flesh and the present Christ together in one and the same perspective. He writes only *one* volume. His framework is that of the life of the incarnate Lord.

Behind this theological perspective lies the great theological conception that the revelation of God in the life of the incarnate Logos is the *climax* of all divine revelation. It is the climax and centre of every saving event which either has taken place *before* this incarnation or will *develop after* the earthly life of Jesus in his community. At the same time the *whole* of the saving event is *concentrated* in this supreme revelation which is comprised in the earthly life of Jesus. This deep conviction determines the purpose of the evangelist. So he connects the historical life of Jesus with the divine revelations which *preceded* it and with those which *follow* it. He connects it with the history of Israel and before that with the first divine revelation in the work of creation. The word of creation, in the beginning, is the very word which has now become flesh at a particular point of time: it is God's communication of himself to the world, revelation. This is the powerful message of the prologue. In addition to this, however, the evangelist connects each particular event with its extension as proclaimed in the community.[9]

The word *ecclesia* does not occur in the Gospel. From this, some scholars have drawn the erroneous conclusion that the author was uninterested in the church. In reality, this interest is stronger in the writer of the Fourth Gospel than in any other evangelist. First of all, of course, the writer is concerned with the special 'Johannine' community, the community to which he and his disciples belong. We may follow Ernst Käsemann in speaking of an *'ecclesiola in ecclesia'*.[10] We shall see how the evangelist is concerned to defend as legitimate the particular form of Christianity which distinguishes his group. He sets out to show that this type of Christianity goes back to the incarnate Jesus in the same way as the other types, and does so in a special way.[11] This helps us to understand better why the evangelist is particularly interested in choosing the characteristic perspective in which he sets the life of Jesus. He means to show that his community really goes back to Jesus, that it was *willed* by Jesus. It is the church of Jesus like any other.

I would, however, differ from Käsemann when he supposes that the author was engaged in direct *polemic* against the mainstream church. This seems to me to be impossible. He never loses sight of the church in its *unity*; indeed, this is one of his most important concerns. As we shall see, the *difference* from Peter, who represents another branch of the church, is *stressed*, but Peter is never *attacked*.

Exegesis will confirm the trend of the above survey. Here I must be content with only a few instances. The narrative about the woman of Samaria in ch. 4 deals with a particular event: the meeting between

Jesus and the woman of Samaria at Jacob's well, which is only attested by the Fourth Gospel. The author feels that this event from the life of the incarnate Jesus prefigures two most important works realized by Christ in his church: the *worship* of the community and its *mission*. Jesus is present in both as he is present in the conversation with the woman of Samaria at Jacob's well. After his declaration about worship 'in spirit and truth', occasioned by the specific problem of the sanctuary on Gerizim ('the hour is coming, and now is', v. 23), he goes on to give a prophetic account of the *mission* in Samaria as it will be carried out first by the Hellenists and then by the apostles. Despite Jesus' command in the synoptic gospels, 'Enter no town of the Samaritans' (Matt. 10.5), which is valid for the period of his earthly life, the *future* mission in Samaria, which is the foundation of *all* mission, is willed by Christ. Indeed, the incarnate Jesus *wishes* it to happen in the time after his death. Its basis is given in the conversation with the woman of Samaria: 'The fields are already white for harvest' (v. 35). It is introduced *after* the resurrection of Christ by the *Hellenists*, by Philip and Stephen's followers, the *alloi* of 4.38, into whose work the other disciples will 'enter'.[12]

We can see the same interest in the coming *mission* of the community on other occasions in the life of Jesus the incarnate: in the saying about the good shepherd (10.16), 'I have other sheep, that are not of this fold'; in the request of the Greeks to see Jesus (12.20f.), in Jesus' answer, which prophetically indicates that the mission to the Gentiles can only begin after his death: 'Unless a grain of wheat . . . dies, it remains alone; but if it dies, it bears much fruit' (v. 24, an image of the mission), and in the same chapter: 'I, when I am lifted up from the earth, will draw *all* men to myself' (12.32).

In other events, the evangelist sees the details of what happened *once* as prefigurements of the *sacraments*. Thus it can be seen that the miracle at Cana (2.1ff.) is also regarded as a prophetic reference to the wine of the eucharist, and the miraculous feeding (6.1ff.) as a reference to the eucharistic bread. John 19.34 mentions the detail of the spear thrust which made blood and water flow from the wounded side of the crucified Jesus, a detail which is almost certainly historical; according to the great majority of interpreters this mention is intended to root the foundation of the eucharist and baptism in the cross of Christ.

The narratives about John the Baptist in the first chapter are meant to demonstrate within the framework of the first 'testimony' to Christ the need for the church to fight, not against John the Baptist, but probably against the assertions of *the Baptist's sect* which proclaimed John as *the* prophet of the end-time or as the Messiah. Other features of the life of Jesus which are stressed in the Gospel tacitly serve to combat another heresy, *docetism*.[13] The Johannine Epistles, whose author is probably a member of the group to which the Fourth Evangelist belongs, also give an urgent warning against this old heresy.

According to this survey, then, the Gospel of John informs us about both the life of Jesus and the early community at the same time. In one of my first publications, *Early Christian Worship*,[14] I was therefore able to use the Gospel of John to draw conclusions about ideas of baptism and eucharist in the ancient church.[15] But worship is only one of the manifestations of the presence of Christ in the church.[16] He is equally at work in mission and in fighting against heretics and unbelieving Jews.

It might now be objected that there is nothing specifically Johannine in the account of the purpose of the Gospel which I have given here. Indeed, one might ask: did not the situation of the early church also influence the *synoptic* gospels? And have the works of the form critics not taught us to understand the faith and life of the church as the occasion for the development of the tradition of the synoptic gospels, as their 'Sitz im Leben'? However, the synoptic tradition is more the collective and *unconscious* work of the first Christians, without a particular deliberate *purpose*. In the case of the Gospel of John, on the other hand, the simultaneous consideration of the incarnate Jesus and the Christ present in the church is the *conscious aim* pursued by an individual author.

This simultaneity, the identity of the incarnate Jesus and the exalted Christ, is often expressed in the Gospel of John by the use of ambiguous expressions. I enumerated a variety of these expressions in an early article.[17] Here I need only mention as an example the verb *hypsothenai*, which in 12.32 means both 'to be lifted up on the cross' and 'to be lifted up to the Father'. 'I, when I am lifted up from the earth, will draw all men to myself'; the next verse declares: 'He said this to show by what death he was to die.'[18]

Even if chs. 15–17 were really inserted by the redactor,[19] the fare-well discourses (13.31ff.) are the key to seeing something of what might be called the self-awareness of the evangelist. He is only capable of grasping the *deeper* meaning of the life of Jesus, 'inspired by the Paraclete', after the death and resurrection of the Lord: as the climax, centre and *concentration* of the whole divine history of salvation. In 16.12 Christ says, 'I have yet many things to say to you, but you cannot bear them now. When the Spirit of truth comes, he will guide you into all the truth.' But only at that moment. And in 14.26 we hear: 'The (Holy) Spirit . . . will teach you all things, and bring to your remembrance all that I have said to you.' This 'call to remembrance'[20] in John certainly also refers to the remembrance of material facts, but in addition it implies more: the understanding of the relationship of the words and deeds of Jesus to the *whole* saving event, and especially to the works which Christ performs through the disciples and of which he says in 14.12: 'He who believes in me will also do the works that I do; and greater works than these will he do, because I go to the Father.' Christ will be exalted, but he is still the one who was on earth with them. The disciples are not left desolate.[21]

In 2.22 we can establish clearly that *mnesthenai* has this double significance in the Gospel. The context here is the cleansing of the temple, which is at the same time an announcement of the replace-ment of the temple by the person of the dead and risen Christ. 'When therefore he was raised from the dead, his disciples remembered that he had said this; and they believed the scripture and the word which Jesus had spoken.' We find the same thing in 12.12ff.: after the author has related the entry of Jesus into Jerusalem to what is written in the Old Testament, he continues, 'His disciples did not under-stand this at first; but when Jesus was glorified, then they *remembered* that this had been written of him and had been done to him' (12.16).

On the ground of this conviction that he is being guided by the Paraclete in this remembrance, the evangelist can allow himself to develop the discourses beyond what the incarnate Jesus said. With-out indicating any transition, he can suddenly introduce his own words (e.g. in 3.13, in the conversation with Nicodemus, where Jesus as incarnate speaks of the one who has ascended into heaven). The risen Christ speaks *through* the evangelist. Through him the Christ continues the teaching which he gave during his incarnation.

Now does this new perspective mean that the Gospel of John cannot be used as a historical source for the life of the earthly Jesus? This question is directly related to the question of the purpose of the Gospel as I believe that I can see it. At the same time, it sheds light on the special traditions or personal reminiscences which were alive in the Johannine circle.

III

THE HISTORICAL VALUE OF
THE FOURTH GOSPEL

W E SHALL FIRST discuss the question of the historical claim
of the Gospel and then see whether this claim is justified.

1. *The claim to factuality*

We have defined the purpose of the evangelist as being both to give
an account of the words and deeds of Jesus and to demonstrate their
significance for the church. It would be wrong to conclude from this,
though, that we may regard the Gospel of John as a historical source
only for knowledge of the *community* to which the author belongs. In
stressing the identity of the incarnate Jesus and the Christ of the
community in the mind of the evangelist, I mean that each of these
expressions should be taken equally seriously.[1] That means that
despite the theological perspective from which he views the life of
Jesus, the evangelist at least makes the *claim* that he is reporting facts
the veracity of which is extremely important to him. For him the
time of the incarnation is the centre, the climax of the divine revelation. He pursues the radiation of this central work of the incarnation
in two directions: forwards into the church (as *throughout* the Gospel),
and backwards as far as creation (as in the prologue). And his perspective is one of salvation history, despite the fact that he contem-
plates the two planes in the life of Jesus the incarnate simultaneously.[2]
His whole enterprise would be senseless if he did not regard the words
and deeds of Jesus as being completely real, since the whole of God's
revelation to the world is *concentrated* in the work which Jesus accomplished during the brief period of his earthly life. It unfolds in both
directions.

Consequently the Johannine account of the life of Jesus cannot be seen so to speak as a purely external framework, a kind of allegory which the author has merely chosen as a literary fiction to express his theological interpretation of Christ. Were that the case, he could have contented himself with expressing his theological notions in the form of a tractate or in epistles like the Johannines. But he wrote a *life of Jesus*, even if it does have a theological slant. For him, the narrative of what happened once is not an outer garment which could be stripped from the Gospel. In this case *history*, *facts*, are the *object* of theological consideration.[3] The equation 'Jesus the incarnate =the church's Christ' demands of the evangelist a careful effort to give a faithful account of what took place during the brief span of Jesus' earthly activity.

We have yet to ask whether he achieved his aim. But first it seems to me important to recognize that at least he *claims* to present facts and not a kind of allegory. According to the evangelist, what was accomplished by Jesus Christ at a quite definite *point in history* and in a quite definite *geographical setting* was preordained in God's plan as the climax and summing up of his revelation. One of the key themes of the entire Gospel is that the decisive *hora*, the 'hour' of Jesus' death, i.e. his glorification, could not be advanced. For this reason, in John Jesus travels to and fro between Galilee and Judaea so that events are not precipitated by a premature arrest and capture. All the other *horai* in the life of Jesus, which the evangelist often gives with astonishing precision – e.g. 1.39: 'it was the tenth hour' – are extraordinarily important with respect to the one hour. Everything that happens in the Gospel narratives takes place according to a fore-ordained divine 'timetable', as one might almost call it. During this brief period of activity every moment is of supreme significance for the salvation of the world.[4]

John 7.1–11 is very instructive in this respect. His brothers, Jesus says in v. 7, are free to arrange their *kairos*. They can go up to Jerusalem at any time they want. Jesus, on the other hand, must wait for the particular moment for each of his works. Verse 6: 'My time has not yet come.' He has to work 'while it is day' (9.4); 'Are there not twelve hours in the day?' (11.9).

Thus according to John 9.2ff. the reason why the blind man has to be *born* blind must be sought not in a sin committed by himself or his parents, but in the divine necessity for Jesus to meet him at this moment and in this particular place to heal him, so that 'the works of God might be made manifest in him' (v. 3). Similarly, in 11.15 Jesus says that he is glad that he was not there before Lazarus died, for had he been there, Lazarus would not have died. In that case Jesus would have performed a healing miracle. But this was the moment for him to perform the miracle of raising Lazarus from the dead: 'For your sake I am glad that I was not there, so that you may believe.' Like the explanation of the blind man, who had to be born blind so that Jesus, the light of the world, might meet him at that moment, this explanation could and had to cause offence, unless the purpose of the evangelist was remembered: he set out to show that everything that happened during Jesus' ministry was the *central* realization of the divine plan of the salvation.

The same may be said of the geographical area of Jesus' activity, of his going to and fro between Judaea and Galilee, and perhaps also of 4.4, where the author says that Jesus *had to* go through Samaria. He had to meet the woman of Samaria there at Jacob's well, whereas the Jews were accustomed to make a detour so as not to have to go through Samaria, which was excommunicated by the Jews. He had to meet the woman in order to prepare the ground for the future mission in Samaria.

2. *Is the claim historically justified?*

The evangelist is evidently convinced that he is reporting facts because he is relying on traditions or reminiscences which appear to him to be certain. However, this does not settle the question whether this claim is justified in the light of historical criticism, whether the Fourth Gospel can be used as a source for the life of Jesus. Many New Testament scholars would answer this question in the negative. They point to the undeniable fact that the Gospel puts history at the service of a theological interest. In fact, we have seen that this is a theological interest in demonstrating the identity between the historical Jesus and the eternal Christ. The evangelist gives a *testimony of faith about history*. The synoptic gospels also do this, however, and in this respect there is no difference in principle between them and the Gospel of John. In fact, we know from both form criticism

and redaction criticism that the synoptic gospels are similarly testi-
monies of faith and not biographies. Yet despite this, modern research into the life of Jesus makes use of them.

We must certainly investigate the character of the testimony of
faith and the precise theological purpose which underlies a gospel,
but this very work should allow us to recognize the historical elements within this testimony.[5]

In our case it is necessary first to recognize the particular theological perspective of the Gospel of John which has been described
above. We have seen that the Gospel is governed by a *deliberate*
intent, and consequently must realize that this has doubtless influenced the *choice* of narratives and sayings more than in the synoptic
gospels; it will also have influenced *the way in which they are presented*.
To deny this would be bad apologetics. Nevertheless, however
great the difference may be between the synoptic perspective and
that of the Fourth Gospel, we are not justified in excluding the latter
as a historical source.

Moreover, there is now a reaction on the part of many very critical
New Testament scholars against a systematic exclusion of the Gospel
as a source about the life of Jesus. A reversal has taken place in this
respect. Thus M. Goguel explicitly also uses the Gospel of John as a
foundation for his book about Jesus, especially the passion narrative,
and C. H. Dodd has devoted an important book to the question of
the historical value of the Johannine tradition.[6]

Although the special traditions at the disposal of the evangelist
within his circle are intended to demonstrate a precise divine plan
within the course of events during the brief activity of Jesus, their
origin and derivation cannot simply be explained by the claim that
they are the creation of the evangelist. Very serious arguments in
favour of a number of historical elements in the Gospel can be supported by exegesis. In particular, I would mention the traditions
which relate to Judaea and Samaria. At first the relationship between Jesus and John the Baptist in *Judaea* is very close: Jesus and his
first disciples are initially still overshadowed by the activity of the
Baptist. One should also note all the references to Samaria; the very
precise details about topography[7] and about Jewish rites; and especially the passion narrative and its chronology, which seems to fit
in with historical reality better than that of the synoptic gospels.

Another important feature is the juristic role played by the Romans, who have much more initiative in a political denunciation than appears in the synoptic gospels: there is the resolution of the Sanhedrin (11.47ff.); the arrest of Jesus by a Roman chiliarch (18.12); the more consultative character of the hearing before the Sanhedrin and the term *titulus* used for the obligatory inscription over the cross, which indicates a political crime. [8]

Even where a redactor has not intervened, the Gospel of course also has passages which are parallel to others in the synoptic gospels. In them we often find that the Gospel of John represents a *later* stage of the tradition than that in the synoptic gospels, in a way which cannot be explained by reference to the Johannine theological perspective.

Both these features should be borne in mind: on the one hand there are some very good historical traditions; on the other, there is a later development in a number of parallel passages. We shall find the explanation for this when we come to speak of the author. At this point no more than a hint need be given. The fact that the more reliable historical traditions (which are even better than those in the synoptic gospels) on the whole relate to events in *Judaea*, will give us the clue. In a later chapter I shall demonstrate that the evangelist was probably not a member of the Twelve and unlike them lived in *Judaea*. We can therefore see how the accounts of early events in *Judaea* and the whole of the passion narrative may rest on personal reminiscences, whereas for other details, especially of events taking place in Galilee, the author relies both on traditions which he has in common with the synoptic gospels and also partly on special traditions, but is not himself an eye-witness.

In connection with the Johannine *discourses* of Jesus, which are so different from the synoptic preaching of the kingdom of God, I have already remarked that the evangelist feels justified in acting in a sovereign manner and himself speaking in the name of Jesus without indicating the transition. We cannot therefore assume as a matter of course that the discourses represent words spoken by Jesus. Nevertheless, in certain cases we must ask whether it is not possible to imagine a more intimate teaching given by Jesus to the Twelve, apart from the preaching to be found in the synoptics, which had a different character. [9]

The question should at least be discussed, as in Matt. 11.25–27 we find, in a synoptic gospel, a saying ('No one knows the Son except the Father') whose '*Johannine*' character is expressly stressed in the commentaries. We shall see that the evangelist belongs to a special circle and is related to a particular form of Judaism lying on its periphery, which we shall examine in connection with the milieu of the Gospel. In the light of this, we must discuss in a later chapter the question of *Jesus*' relationship to this .non-conformist marginal Judaism and his relationship to the 'Johannine circle'. Even if we cannot give a complete answer, at least the question must be raised seriously.

To deny an almost certain influence of the evangelist's theological perspective on his choice of events and the way in which they are described, together with the continued development of certain traditions, with the illusory aim of rescuing the integral historicity of *all* the details of the Gospel of John, is a perverse piece of apologetics. But it is equally perverse to deny any historical value at all to the Gospel of John because of the theological perspectives in which events are shown. Our findings are confirmed. The importance to the evangelist of the theological statement that 'the historical Jesus and the Christ present in the community are one' must have been a stimulus to him to portray the words and deeds of the first member of this expression of identity, the incarnate Jews, as faithfully as possible. This does not, of course, mean that we may expect him to have exercised critical control over traditions which he used about events of which he was not an eye-witness.

IV

LANGUAGE, STYLE AND
LITERARY CHARACTERISTICS

THE PROBLEM of Johannine language and Johannine style has a
different aspect, depending on whether we begin by distinguishing sources and redactions or treat the Gospel as a whole. Thus
Bultmann assumes that both the *semeia* source and the passion narrative were written in a Greek heavily permeated by Semitisms,
whereas the original language of the revelation discourses was
Aramaic. The style of the revelation discourses is, he believes,
stamped by the literary genre of gnostic revelations. But even here,
despite very good insights, the distinction seems to me to be rather
too schematic, not to mention problematical, seeing that detailed
examinations have led to contrary results. Here too, therefore, we
shall speak of the language and style of the Gospel as such, leaving
open the question whether it has been influenced by certain sources
and redactions. The latter must be discussed at individual points in
the exegesis.

Up to the first decades of the twentieth century, modern critical
works exclusively assigned the Fourth Gospel to the Hellenistic
sphere; the question whether its Greek language presupposed a
Semitic original or at least betrayed Semitic influence was usually
ignored completely. There were few exceptions to this view, of whom
A. Schlatter deserves special mention. As early as 1902 he thought
that a comparison with the Midrash demonstrated the presence of
numerous Hebraisms in the gospel, which suggested to him that the
author came from Palestine.[1] An investigation by K. Beyer pointing
to analogies with the Qumran texts, which were also composed in
Hebrew, arrived at a similar result at a much later date.[2]

C. F. Burney directed attention to Aramaic and assumed on the basis of a detailed philological investigation that the Gospel as we have it is virtually a translation from Aramaic.[3] He even believed that he could point to mistakes in the translation.[4] C. C. Torrey took this approach further,[5] and while J. de Zwaan[6] and M. Black[7] avoid some of Burney's exaggerations, they come to similar conclusions: the former also presupposes an Aramaic original, and the latter believes that the Gospel was written for the most part in Greek, with a strong Aramaic influence. Despite the criticisms made by E. C. Colwell,[8] this latter view has gained more and more ground. We have seen that Bultmann supposes that the sources which he posits had a more or less obviously Aramaic background.

On reading the Gospel one gains the impression that the language is generally Semitic, although on closer inspection some similarities with Hebrew can also be found in Koine Greek and in the Septuagint: the rare appearance of subordinate clauses, the placing of the verb before the subject (ἀνέβη εἰς ʽΙεροσόλυμα ὁ ʼΙησοῦς), the repetition of the personal pronoun, and so on.

The various philological observations about Hebrew and Aramaic influence made by the scholars mentioned above (e.g. the Aramaic ן which corresponds both to the Greek final conjunction and to the Greek relative pronoun ἵνα, raising the possibility of errors in translation) are very important, but they do not justify the conclusion drawn by C. F. Burney and C. C. Torrey that the Gospel is a direct translation from the Aramaic. In reality, the philological remarks only demonstrate that the author came from a milieu in which the use of Aramaic was common. Following K. Beyer, R. Schnackenburg has assembled in his commentary a series of expressions which the Gospel shares with the Qumran texts.[9] Quite apart from this question, E. A. Abbott investigated the characteristics of Johannine vocabulary (and style) in a much older work.[10]

It has often rightly been stressed that the language of the Gospel of John is somewhat monotonous. This seems deliberate, and is reminiscent of liturgical style, which is not afraid of repetitions. Related to this is the fact that the thought of the Gospel is not developed in direct progressions; the same truth is considered from different perspectives. Another reason for the monotony is perhaps that the content of the whole Gospel follows a single aim. On the other hand, the remarkable style is probably also influenced by the theological conceptions which we find in a certain kind of non-conformist Judaism, from which lines can be drawn to an earlier stage of gnosticism. This is a subject to be discussed later.

It is probable that some parts of the Gospel have been composed in a rhythmic style. This is almost certain in the case of the prologue, and applies to other places also. Several scholars have used the rules of Hebrew poetry to define the rhythm, the alternation of strophes and the parallelism of Johannine style more closely. Bultmann posits a source of revelation discourses in the Gospel which, according to him, has preserved the poetic form of the discourses P. Gaechter, in particular, has attempted to describe the forms of Johannine poetry.[11] A number of modern translations, e.g. the French 'Jerusalem' Bible[12] and that made by R. E. Brown, have divided the Greek text into strophes and marked this division in typographical form. These proposals for reconstructing Johannine rhythm and the Johannine strophes do, however, seem to me to be burdened with too many subjective and hypothetical elements.[13] Moreover, the various solutions discussed here clash with one another, and their hypothetical character is even more noticeable if one follows some scholars in their attempt to go back to an Aramaic original. At all events, there are problems in moving to a division of sources and an identification of additions from considerations of rhythm.

We have already mentioned the use of ambiguous expressions in the Gospel.[14] This is very characteristic, and accords well with the particular perspective in which the life of Jesus is seen in conjunction with the work of the Christ present in the church. Many other instances can be cited in addition to the verb *hypsothenai*, which has already been discussed.[15]

A number of constant features in the development of the dialogue are also connected with the purpose followed by the author: the incomprehension of those with whom Jesus speaks, their inability to move from one sense of a word or expression to another,[16] and in other cases their initial doubt, which ends in faith.

I have already made numerous references to the explicit character of the discourses of Jesus: they often continue a dialogue occasioned by a specific situation in the life of Jesus, while completely forgetting the occasion which prompted them. Thus it comes about that the person involved in conversation with Jesus can completely vanish from the scene whereas the discourse of Jesus continues. This can be noted, for instance, in the conversation with Nicodemus.

The theological perspective also explains the Johannine manner of narrating events, which is very different from that of the synoptic gospels. We do not always have a very specific conception of the scene as a whole. Some aspects are described with a surprising amount of detail, whereas others are completely ignored, so that the narrative as a whole remains vague. It is as though a spotlight illuminated just one part of a picture with great brilliance, while the rest of it remained in shadow. Then the spotlight moves to another part of the same picture, but without any obvious connection with what went before. This often gives the narratives in John their somewhat mysterious character. The evangelist is only interested in those aspects of events which demonstrate links with the Christ present in the church. As soon as he has communicated what is important in this respect, he moves on to another narrative.

Language, style and literary characteristics may thus be explained primarily in terms of the theological aim of the evangelist, though they are also shaped by the conceptions of the Johannine circle which are determined by the particular milieu in which he is rooted.

V

THE NON-CHRISTIAN ENVIRONMENT OF
THE GOSPEL AND THE JOHANNINE CIRCLE

THE QUESTION of the environment of the Gospel of John has long been put in the form of an alternative: 'Hellenism or Judaism?' The more parallels to Johannine conceptions and concepts have been discovered in the literature of Hellenism, the more scholars have refrained from drawing on Jewish sources. The affinity between Johannine theology and Jewish Hellenism as represented by Philo of Alexandria, whose Logos doctrine is analogous to that of John, for all the differences, made it possible to consider a link between the Jewish theory and the Hellenistic theory. However, this reference to Philo was not enough to decide the alternatives. For Philo does not belong to Palestinian Judaism. A new alternative therefore arose: Palestinian Judaism or the Hellenistic Judaism of the diaspora?

However, over recent decades new research and especially the discovery of new sources have brought about a revolution in this respect. These demonstrate that even the alternative of Palestinian Judaism or the Hellenistic Judaism of the diaspora is a false one. The Palestinian Judaism of the New Testament period was much less homogeneous than had been supposed when historians had been content to follow the synoptic gospels in dividing Jews exclusively into Pharisees and Sadducees. In reality this Palestinian Judaism was infinitely more varied. Earlier investigations into apocalyptic had already drawn attention to more or less esoteric circles in Palestine in which an eschatological hope was cherished which at some points showed signs of a foreign origin. On the other hand, it became clear that in these or kindred circles there were speculations about the origin of the world in connection with Old Testament narratives, which reveal equally varied arguments akin to Hellenism.

There was, therefore, already a theory that sectarian groups were to be found on the borders of Palestinian Judaism. Research into Samaritan religion also helped to arouse interest in the encounter between syncretism and Palestinian Judaism. Above all, however, the discovery of the Qumran texts confirmed the intensive vigour of a heterodox movement whose importance for understanding Palestinian Judaism in the time of Jesus is to be accounted very high.[1] It is becoming more and more evident that faithfulness to the traditions of Judaism did not exclude openness to alien influences. Thus some syncretistic tendencies are by no means just a particular phenomenon of the Greek diaspora. They were restricted to this role by earlier scholars, but in fact they were particularly marked in Palestine and Syria.[2]

The architecture of the temple of Herod in Jerusalem, with the strong Greek influence on it, may have assumed its form for a variety of reasons, but it is so to speak the outward symbol of the recognition that the thought of Hellenism, too, stamped Palestinian Judaism at the time of Jesus far more profoundly than has been assumed.

As early as 1930, in my investigation of the old Jewish-Christian source the *Kerygmata Petrou*, embodied in the Pseudo-Clementines,[3] I drew attention to the affinity of heretical Jewish Christianity to *this* Judaism, and suggested that this heterodox Judaism – I called it 'gnostic' – should be seen as one of the sources of Christianity. This theory becomes particularly relevant in the light of the question of the environment of the Gospel of John. As long as it was thought that the origin of the Gospel of John had to be sought as far as possible outside the Palestinian sphere and as long as the starting point was the alternative between Judaism and Hellenism, only a group of scholars attempted to relate the Gospel to non-conformist Judaism; this approach did not yet enter the mainstream of Johannine scholarship. The commentaries of W. Bauer and R. Bultmann brought about a decisive change here.

However, the conviction also increasingly gained ground that Old Testament influence is by no means lacking in the Gospel, and this led to a revision of the academic presupposition which had so

long dominated Johannine scholarship. Of course it must be conceded that Old Testament passages are rarely cited in the Gospel of
John, but the references to Old Testament themes are much more
numerous, especially those related to the book of Exodus. References are rightly made by scholars to the wisdom literature.[4] The
proximity to Palestinian Judaism is suggested by further observations. After Schlatter,[5] C. H. Dodd in particular stressed the
numerous points of contact with rabbinic Judaism in his book on
the interpretation of the Fourth Gospel.[6] Many instances can be
found in exegesis. On the other hand, the Gospel shows itself to
be very familiar with the topography of Jerusalem and with Jewish
worship and Jewish customs.[7]

As early as 1929, H. Odeberg in particular investigated 'Jewish
mysticism', and thus associated the Gospel directly with the esoteric
Judaism in which so many syncretistic tendencies meet.[8] For want of
a better expression, and aware of the difficulty of finding a fully
appropriate term, in the remarks which follow I shall term this
Judaism 'non-conformist' or even 'heterodox Judaism', 'marginal
Judaism'. In my earlier studies I called it 'esoteric' or even 'gnostic';
this is not inappropriate for what is in any case a prelude to gnosticism, but it does not do justice to the whole phenomenon.[9]

It is here that we shall look for the origin of the so-called Hellenism of the Fourth Gospel.[10] The exegetes who formerly thought for
apologetic reasons that they should deny any Hellenistic influence
on Johannine theology are wrong, but so are those who in contrast,
faithful to their critical independence, thought that they had to
contest the undeniable familiarity of the evangelist with Palestinian
Judaism.

In turn, this non-conformist Judaism has numerous roots in the
pagan syncretism of its environment. It is impossible, therefore, to
draw sharp lines between this Judaism and gnostic tendencies. All
the streams of Oriental and Hellenistic syncretism in this period,
whether they are found in Palestine or Syria or the Greek diaspora,
are related, and although they take different forms depending on the
characteristics of the areas or the civilizations in which they are
found, they have influenced one another, or all go back to a common source. Many of the documents attesting this syncretism are
probably later than the beginnings of Christianity, but the themes

dealt with in them show considerable continuity, and some of these themes could be much older than the documents in which they are contained. For this reason the current practice[11] of seeking parallels between the Gospel of John and gnosticism, the Hermetic literature and Mandaeanism is by no means unjustified, even if the sources in which these parallels are thought to occur come from the Christian period and from areas outside Palestine. Still, some caution should be exercised in using writings of too late a date. The possibility must be considered that they have been influenced by the Gospel of John and not vice versa; the views developed in them could in fact derive from the Gospel itself.

At all events, in principle use should first be made of sources which certainly come from pre-Christian times; the others should only be considered as secondary sources, and provided that they demonstrate the same tendencies. In this context a special place must be assigned to the *Qumran scrolls*. The almost unending literature on these writings and their relationship to earliest Christianity relates for the most part to the Gospel of John in particular. Here I mention only a few names like those of F. M. Braun,[12] G. Baumbach,[13] Herbert Braun,[14] K. G. Kuhn,[15] O. Betz[16] and J. Roloff.[17] These scholars have investigated the related views of the Qumran sect and Johannine theology. Various fundamental conceptions have been compared, particularly 'dualism'[18] and the idea of the 'spirit'.[19]

The role of ritual ablutions in the Qumran community and in sectarian Judaism generally,[20] their sacred meals, their criticism of the temple and priesthood at Jerusalem are definitely to be considered as a background for certain liturgical ideas in the Gospel of John. Of course this does not leave out of account important differences between the Johannine conception of the abolition of the temple, and baptism and eucharist in the Gospel on the one hand, and the Qumran criticism of the temple and its corresponding rites on the other. It is impossible to answer with any certainty the question whether we may also assume a *historical* connection between the two, perhaps going through John the Baptist and his disciples. In any event, however, it is probable that despite his independence and his own different character, John the Baptist belongs in the *milieu* of the Jewish baptist movement and the special conceptions associated with it.[21] In this way these views may have influenced the Johannine circle. The close connection between the Gospel of John and the disciples of the Baptist, to whom the author probably belonged, can hardly be disputed.[22]

Scholars had in fact connected the *baptist sect* with the Gospel of John long before the discovery of the Dead Sea scrolls. It is to the credit of Bultmann,[23] basing his work on the extremely illuminating remarks of W. Baldensperger,[24] that he directed the attention of Johannine research to the role of this sect in his much-studied article of 1925. At the same time, he stressed their connection with the Mandaeans, whose sacred writings had at that time been made available to a wider audience thanks to Lidzbarski's translation. In these writings John the Baptist sometimes appears as an ambassador. During the two decades which immediately followed, through the twenties and thirties, with few exceptions almost all works on John were dominated by the Mandaean question. At that time M. Goguel spoke of a Mandaean fever which had seized New Testament scholars. The two great commentaries which appeared in 1930 and 1941, by W. Bauer and especially that by R. Bultmann, introduce many quotations from the Mandaean writings.

It must be granted that even if these documents are not pre-Christian in their present form, like the Qumran scrolls, they at least belong in the same sphere as the Jewish baptist sects, and that for the reasons given above the objections made against their use on the grounds of the very late date of the last strata are not *a priori* justified. Nevertheless, it is true that the Mandaeans were cited somewhat indiscriminately as parallels to the Gospel of John, and distinctions were not always made between the different strata. By contrast, H. Lietzmann believed that they were of no value for the understanding of the New Testament environment. Now, however, new texts have been edited by Lady Drower, and the more recent fundamental work of K. Rudolph has shown on the basis of them that the Mandaeans originated in pre-Christian times in the region of Palestine.[25] Of course, Rudolph denies any connection between the Mandaeans and the sect of John the Baptist.[26] But the assumption that the later baptist sects and the Mandaeans at least belong to a common *environment* is supported by the discovery that on the one hand important Mandaean concepts occur in the Gospel of John and on the other, the first chapters contain an obvious and undeniable polemic against a sect which saw John the Baptist as its Messiah or at least as the eschatological prophet (*Pseudo-Clementine Recognitions* I, 54–60; see also Luke 3.15).

Bultmann, in particular, attaches great significance to the influence of the Mandaean redeemer myth on Johannine theology. He sees this myth as an expression of the more general gnostic myth, also attested in other systems, of which R. Reitzenstein had already spoken.[27] Mandaeanism does in fact belong in the milieu which is usually described as gnostic, in which this myth has its home. However, the Mandaean texts know a number of 'heavenly ambassadors', and not just one. Some Johannine formulations certainly hint at such concepts and ideas, and although it is impossible to establish a direct historical derivation, it can be concluded that through the mediation of a certain kind of Judaism, the Gospel of John is in contact with at least a kindred world of ideas.

How far the term 'gnostic' may be used only in connection with the 'redeemer myth'[28] is a problem in itself. It refers primarily to redemption through 'gnosis'. The discussion of terminology is unending. We have already seen that the Gospel of John as a whole has also been termed 'gnostic'. This is correct in that the heterodox Judaism from which the Gospel derives displays *pre-gnostic* features. This is why the Gospel was particularly highly valued in gnostic circles. But the affinity with syncretistic and even gnostic ideas in any case hardly justifies the connection. Bornkamm's conclusion, that the Gospel of John 'is directed towards a gnostic world of ideas and that this also brings out its difference from gnosticism',[29] is correct.

At any rate, the 'redeemer myth' is not to be assigned the dominant role in the explanation of Johannine christology accorded to it by Rudolf Bultmann and his pupils, simply because of the use of kindred concepts in the Gospel of John.[30] This fails to do justice to the christological themes which are specifically to be derived from early Christian faith. In defining the milieu of the Gospel and its theological position within primitive Christianity, however, the conceptual parallels drawn by these scholars retain their value. We should also mention here the question how far the Jewish concepts of 'wisdom' and the divine Word are connected with this redeemer myth.[31]

A general warning ought to be issued against supposing that in any comparison between Johannine theology and gnosticism the only explanation of *all* the points of contact is that the Gospel of John has been influenced by particular gnostic conceptions. We have already mentioned the possibility that because the gnostic documents are generally late they may in fact be dependent on the Gospel of John; quite apart from this, we may also ask whether each did not influence the other. There are analogies, and in the last resort these go back to a *common milieu*. Cross-connections, especially those between the various heterodox Jewish sects, also point in this direction.[32] It is inevitable that we cannot define the milieu of the Johannine circle as *specifically* as we might wish, and does not detract from a general account of its sphere of origin.

The Odes of Solomon provide one instance of the difficulty of any further explanation of the relationship of the Gospel of John to its environment.[33] They offer such striking parallels that it has often been assumed that they derive from the Gospel of John. However, the presence of an affinity between the Odes of Solomon and the Qumran Hodayot[34] seems rather to suggest their independence from the Gospel, and as it is also improbable that the evangelist made direct use of the Odes, the solution must be sought in a common cultural milieu. If the Syriac in which most of the Odes are written is really original, this would also be a pointer in the same direction, since it is geographically close to the non-conformist Judaism in which the Gospel of John is rooted.

Reference to the pagan literature of the Revelations of Hermes Trismegistos, which has been investigated in detail by A. J. Festugière,[35] can also be valuable in some cases.[36] However, here again, if we can really assume that the work has been revised in a Christian direction (F. M. Braun), we have the question whether the Gospel may itself have influenced this literature. Be that as it may, here too the similarities (e.g. Logos, second birth) suggest a common sphere.

When we think of *Christian* gnosticism, we should think first of the *Jewish-Christian* gnosticism of the pseudo-Clementines,[37] because it is closely related to the whole of non-conformist Judaism. In second place come the Coptic manuscripts discovered at Nag Hammadi. They evidently made use of Christian books, and it seems more natural here than elsewhere to derive the numerous parallels from a direct dependence on the Gospel of John. In many cases, however, we should also consider a pre-Christian origin, and the most important documents in the library, the Gospel of Truth,[38] the Apocryphon of John and the Gospel of Philip,[39] have been compared with the Gospel of John from this perspective.

On the other hand, insufficient use has been made of the more recent studies of *Samaritan* religion in seeking to understand certain Johannine conceptions, although this religion is in some respects especially close both to the Gospel of John and to heterodox Judaism. The sources: the Samaritan Pentateuch, the chronicles, the liturgy and the work Memar by the Samaritan Marqah from the fourth century AD,[40] have been made available in modern editions, and the literature about this remarkable community, which claims to be the guardian of the authentic traditions of Israel, although it is separated from official Judaism, has grown considerably in recent years. In addition to the general works about Samaritan religion by M. Gaster[41] and more recently by J. Macdonald,[42] a large number of important monographs appear each year.[43]

For reasons which I can only discuss in the next chapter, it seems to me indispensable to pay more attention to the Samaritans in this discussion of the milieu of the Gospel of John, as they shed special light on both heterodox Judaism and the Johannine circle. In many respects Samaritanism seems to me to be just as important a syncretistic trend in relation to the background of the Gospel of John as some other gnostic phenomena which have been mentioned and are so often cited in commentaries. Perhaps it is even more so. Like the Qumran sect, it has the advantage of introducing us not only to particular speculations and forms of belief but also to the social and liturgical structures in which they belong; it also has the advantage that Samaritans can be shown to have lived in Palestine in the time of the New Testament.[44] In two articles which appeared in 1953/54 and 1958/59, I drew attention to the significance of the mission in Samaria for Johannine studies in the context of establishing a triangular relationship between heterodox Judaism, the Hellenists in Acts and the Gospel of John.[45] Other scholars, and particularly specialists in Samaritan religion, investigated further in this direction and in particular compared the theological conceptions of the Gospel of John with those of the Samaritans. We shall discuss their important studies in the next chapter.[46]

We reach the conclusion, then, that the milieu of the Gospel is to be seen as a Judaism influenced by syncretism in the area of Palestine and Syria. The home ground of the Johannine circle is to be sought here. I conjectured earlier that the way in which the Gospel speaks in so many places of 'the Jews' as a collective enemy could derive from the terminology which heterodox communities applied to official Judaism.[47]

VI

THE PLACE OF THE JOHANNINE CIRCLE
WITHIN EARLY CHRISTIANITY

THE QUESTIONS which we discussed in the previous chapter are examined in all commentaries and all Johannine studies. But they are exclusively concerned with the *non-Christian* milieu. It would be wrong to think that this settled the question of the Johannine circle, as though it were just one link in the long chain of the 'syncretistic' movement. In reality, the affinity of certain ideas of this circle to syncretism in no way leads to such a conclusion. Despite its undeniable associations, which must certainly be taken into account in making its cultural milieu more precise, the Gospel of John is not simply a product of gnostic syncretism. A conclusion of this kind would imply a historical approach which could not be applied to the beginnings of Christianity, especially as in the theological perspective of the Gospel of John, which also makes use of historical traditions about his life, the activity of Jesus goes beyond the framework of this syncretistic movement, no matter how far the movement itself may also have been influenced by certain expressions of the faith awakened by Jesus. An investigation of the Jewish and pagan milieu cannot release us from the task of fitting the Gospel, with its distinct character, into the rise of Christianity. What Harnack rightly called the great historical riddle of the beginnings of Christianity cannot be explained without an answer to this question. There is a Johannine type as well as a synoptic and a Pauline (or Deutero-Pauline) type, and its origin cannot be sought simply outside the constitutive elements of early Christianity.

Nor can the character of this expression of Christianity simply be attributed to the individuality of the evangelist. Of course his strong personality must be considered in every connection. We have seen that he above all is the creator of the basic conception of the Johannine account of the life of Jesus. But behind him there must have been a group of Christians who not only possessed special traditions about Jesus but also had a belief in his person and work which had particular distinguishing features. An examination of the literary unity of the Gospel already suggests the existence of a Johannine group, if not of a Johannine 'school' proper. The relationship between the Gospel and the Johannine epistles, which beyond doubt indicates that the authors were closely connected, but not necessarily the same, also raises the problem of the existence of a 'Johannine circle'.

Käsemann rightly stresses that this was a community.[1] But in calling this community 'gnostic' and 'docetic' he removes it completely, not only from the historical Jesus but also from the rest of early Christianity. All the points we have made so far lead us, however, to assume a link with what we know about the early church. This community as such is more than a 'primitive Christian community forced into a corner'.[2] We shall see that there is other evidence in the New Testament for the type which it represents in addition to the Gospel of John and the Johannine Epistles.

The history of Christianity in the first century is all too often described exclusively after the pattern of the distinction between the Jewish Christianity of Palestine and the Gentile Christianity of the diaspora. In theory, the Hegelian scheme which the Tübingen school applied to early Christianity has been given up. But in practice people are still more or less under its influence. In terms of this pattern there used to be a preference for assigning the Gospel of John to the Gentile Christianity of the diaspora. But to think of an exclusive contrast between Jewish Christianity and Gentile Christianity is to make the same error as that indicated in the previous chapter: to think of a non-Hellenistic Judaism in Palestine and a Hellenistic Judaism in the diaspora. Just as Palestinian *Judaism* cannot be seen as a homogeneous entity to set over against the Hellenistic Judaism of the diaspora, so Gentile *Christianity* cannot be set over against a homogeneous Jewish *Christianity* in Palestine. E. Lohmeyer already stressed the need to distinguish between the Christians of Galilee and the Christians of Judaea,[3] but it is important to make even further distinctions within the Jewish Christianity of Palestine.

As there was not only an official Judaism in *Palestine* in the New Testament period but also a heterodox Judaism which contained alien elements, we must begin by asking whether nascent Christianity did not reflect this *Jewish* situation. Were the first Christians really recruited only from members of *official* Judaism? On the face of things, this is improbable. As the Gospel of John has considerable affinity with non-conformist Judaism, we must consider whether there was not also a group or groups in the earliest church in Jerusalem who derived from this Judaism and after their conversion stood apart from the other followers of Christ, who were adherents of official Judaism. Do we have direct reports of the presence of such a group in Palestine?

This question must be answered in the affirmative unless we deny that Acts has any historical value at all for a knowledge of the beginnings of Christianity—and despite the need for us to take into account Luke's theological interests, this latter position seems to me to be untenable. The group concerned is that of the 'Hellenists', mentioned by the author of Acts in ch. 6, where they are contrasted with the 'Hebraists' (6.1ff.). Most scholars are agreed that these Hellenists are not simply to be regarded as people who spoke Greek. The verb *hellenizein* means to 'live' (and even to 'think') in a Greek manner. The designation does not tell us much about the character of the group,[4] but it does denote a special group which was more open to foreign influences and adopted a freer attitude to the Jewish law and the temple cult than the other members of the early church. I cannot discuss the question of the Hellenists in detail at this point. I have discussed it in passages in a number of my articles,[5] and M. Simon has also made a thorough examination of the subject.[6] At this point I must limit myself to the essential features of the argument.

According to Luke, these Hellenists belonged to the primitive community from the very beginning. This fact is important. They must therefore have represented a *Judaism* of a special kind even *before* they joined the Christian community, and there is nothing to prevent our supposing that some of them were *even followers of Jesus during his lifetime.*

According to Acts, the 'Seven' were chosen and entrusted with 'serving tables' only after a conflict between Hellenists and Hebrews. Luke himself, however, has preserved traces of the recollection that their role was in fact much more important, since he goes on to speak of their activity in preaching. At an earlier stage, they must have been the leaders of the group of Christian Hellenists within the earliest community. Their authority seems to have been analogous to that of the Twelve, though they were also in some way subordinate to the latter. Stephen will be the most representative of the Seven.

To defend himself against the charge of speaking against the temple and changing the law, he delivers an extremely bold speech in which he charges the Jews with having themselves transgressed the law of Moses; he even goes so far as to depict Solomon's building of the temple in Jerusalem as the height of their unfaithfulness, after a brief mention of the making of the golden calf (Acts 7.41–48). These views, which to Jews were blasphemous in the extreme, were evidently shared by the entire Hellenist group,[7] for after Stephen's martyrdom the Jews expelled all the members of the group from Jerusalem, although the Twelve were allowed to remain there (Acts 8.1).[8] From this we may conclude with confidence that the preaching of the Hellenists was different from that of the Hebrews who remained faithful to the temple and gave the Jews no occasion for persecuting them.

The author of Acts tends to pass over or minimize differences among the first Christians, but he has preserved the recollection that the leaders of the earliest community in Jerusalem regarded with some mistrust the missionary activity of these Hellenists in Samaria and in the other areas to which they moved after their persecution. The preaching of the Hellenists in Samaria was crowned with success: the Samaritans believed and came to be baptized (Acts 8.4ff.). Nevertheless, in v. 14 Luke adds that the Jerusalem community sent Peter and John to Samaria to lay hands on the Samaritans.[9] We shall find that the same thing happens later: the area round *Joppa* is first evangelized by Philip (Acts 8.40), but *Peter* follows him there (9.32ff.): the Hellenists preach the gospel in Antioch and the Jerusalem community then sends *Barnabas* there (Acts 11.19, 22). On his last journey to Jerusalem Paul is extremely anxious about his reception by the leaders of Jewish Christianity, and so he first visits

Philip, one of the Seven (21.8). According to this we have a quite distinct group within Palestinian Judaism.

We have more than general considerations to indicate a very close connection, if not a complete identity, between the *Hellenists in Jerusalem and the Johannine group*. These two groups are remarkably similar in three respects:

1. In theological conceptions. These include their christology and their conception of liturgy, above all of the setting of worship, which we can infer from Stephen's speech and the Gospel of John, though we must note that Stephen's speech gives only a brief outline of this theology, which is adapted to the context of a speech in his defence, whereas the Gospel of John develops the same themes in every direction in the light of belief in Christ;

2. In an interest in the mission to Samaria. Acts 8 and John 4.31ff. show that both have this in common;

3. In the common roots of Stephen's speech and the Gospel of John in heterodox Judaism, above all in Samaritan theology.

We shall now investigate these three points in detail.

1. The theological conceptions common to the Hellenists and the Johannine circle

Stephen's speech can give us some idea of the *theology* of the Hellenists. True, we must take into account the influence of Luke's theology on the speeches in Acts in general. However, Stephen's speech is so far removed from Luke's conceptions and even his language that we must assume that Luke either had a source or at any rate is using a tradition which comes from Stephen's circle.[10] By a survey of Israel's history and its unfaithfulness he shows in ch. 7 that the decisive revelations of God are not bound up with a *country* or a particular *place*.[11] The tabernacle was the ideal place for worshipping the divine presence because it could be moved and did not bind God to a particular place (v. 44). As has already been mentioned, the great apostasy was that of Solomon, who built God a house (v. 48).

According to the speech in Acts 7, it is not Stephen, but his accusers, who are unfaithful to the law. Moses is the prototype of Christ, Deut. 18.15: 'I will raise up for you a prophet like him' (v.

37), a passage which is so often also quoted by heterodox Jews and the Pseudo-Clementines. It is particularly significant for the christology of the speech. At the same time, Jesus is called 'the righteous one' (v. 52). According to what is probably also a Hellenist source in Luke's possession, when his speech is ended (v. 56) Stephen declares that he sees the heavens open and the *'Son of Man standing'* at the right hand of God, evidently as an intercessor for Stephen. This view is not Lukan.

If we compare this theology with that of John, we can see that the leading idea in Acts 7 corresponds exactly with the answer given by Jesus to the question raised by the woman of Samaria. Worship is freed from connections with any particular place; it is 'neither in Gerizim nor in Jerusalem', but 'in spirit and in truth' (John 4.21ff.). We can, however, find the same ideas even in the prologue: the glory, the *doxa*, the Shekinah, which for the Jews was associated with the temple,[12] has detached itself from there and is now visible 'among us' in the person of Christ. The verb *eskenosen*, John 1.14, is indeed a direct allusion to the *skene*, the tabernacle, which according to Stephen's speech is the place of worship desired by God, because it is not fixed in a particular place. Now, however, according to the evangelist, even this has been done away with by Christ, just as according to Rev. 21.22 there is no temple in the future heavenly city because 'God and the Lamb is its temple', though in v. 3 of the same chapter it is said that the *skene* of God will be with men and that he will 'tabernacle' among them. According to the theory of H. H. Schäder,[13] the word *eskenosen* was chosen in John 1.14 because the sound of it (if not the etymology) recalled the Shekinah, the divine *doxa*, which is now seen in the incarnate Jesus. The end of the first chapter of John, v. 51, makes a direct allusion to the story of Jacob's dream at Bethel (Gen. 28). From now on, however, the ladder by which the angels ascend and descend between heaven and earth is no longer in a particular place; the ascent and descent is supported by the Son of Man. It is he who from now on forms the bridge between heaven and earth and manifests the presence of God, and not the stone of Bethel.[14] In the story of the cleansing of the temple in ch. 2 it is again the person of Christ which takes the place of the temple, in connection with the saying about destroying the temple and building it again in three days, which is connected with his body (2.21). This idea reaches a climax in the first part of the dialogue with the woman of Samaria, which has already been mentioned (ch. 4).[15]

The interest of both the Gospel and the Epistles of John in baptism and the eucharist[16] may be connected with the same idea of the abolition of the temple through Christ.[17] Christian worship now concentrates on these as the place where Christ is present. It is impossible to put a precise date on the composition of the Fourth Gospel,[18] but even if the temple was no longer standing by then, the rejection of any association with a particular place – Jerusalem or Gerizim – links the Gospel very closely with the circle around Stephen.

However, unlike the Gospel of John, Stephen's speech only argues the negative aspect: it is opposed to any fixed location for the cult. The positive addition – Christ taking the place of the temple – seems to be absent from the theology of Stephen and his circle. If we keep to the content of the speech, Stephen does not in fact appear to have followed the Gospel in binding worship to the person of Christ. We should not, however, forget that Acts 7 is a speech for the defence, which is delivered before Jews as an answer to their charges. Stephen's preaching, and the preaching of his successors, Philip and his followers, after Stephen's death, was probably not very different from the Johannine message of the abolition of the temple cult through belief in Christ. After all, what else could they preach as believers in Christ in connection with their challenge to temple worship?

The Gospel of John and Stephen's speech not only share the same theology of the place where worship is to be offered but also have contacts in christology. The comparison between Moses and Christ in the Fourth Gospel has long been stressed,[19] and it is also a characteristic of Stephen's speech. The designation 'Son of Man' appears particularly frequently in the Gospel of John.[20] If we follow G. Bornkamm in associating the Son of Man with the Paraclete,[21] the idea of the Son of Man in John is perhaps connected with the Son of Man 'standing' at the right hand of God to make intercession, whom Stephen sees at the end of his speech (Acts. 8.56).

It is also significant that at the very point where the two groups seem to have theological notions in common, lines can be drawn from both Stephen's speech and the Gospel of John to heterodox Judaism. This affords astonishing confirmation of the theory of a connection between the Hellenists and the Johannine circle. The various syncretistic movements mentioned in the previous chapter come under consideration here. However, this heterodox Judaism in its Samaritan form exercised the strongest influence on both Stephen's speech and on the Gospel of John, even if this influence was not exclusive.[22] This is already clear in the example of the inter-cessory Son of Man, mentioned above, which has a parallel in the *intercessory* Moses of Samaritan theology. We shall have to discuss even more striking points of contact in due course.

First of all, however, we shall attempt to answer the question why the influence of the Samaritan form of heterodox Judaism on the two groups is particularly evident.

2. *The common interest of the Hellenists and the Gospel of John in the mission in Samaria*

In due course we shall be discussing the English works devoted to the question which has just been raised. It should be noted that al-most all their explanations begin by taking into account a theological influence exercised by already converted Christian Samaritans on Stephen or his group and on the Johannine circle. I would also assume such an influence, but I consider it to be only a secondary stage of development. Primarily, both external circumstances and the theology fashioned by heterodox Judaism in general *even before the mission* to the Samaritans seem to me to have aroused a strong *missionary* interest among the Hellenists and in the group standing behind the Gospel of John, which naturally directed both these groups towards Samaria. There is another close link between them here, in addition to their liturgical and christological views.

A priori, their ideas, rooted in marginal Judaism, had much in common with Samaritan religion as well as with all the non-con-formist tendencies in Palestine. Thus we can easily understand how the Hellenists, after their expulsion from Jerusalem (Acts 8.1ff.), directed their proclamation of Christ towards Samaria. Here those who were persecuted because of their rejection of the temple cult found a point of contact. For although the Samaritans (unlike the

Hellenists and the Johannine circle) rejected only the temple in Jerusalem, and not all connections with any place of worship whatsoever, they were a ready audience for preaching about the divine presence made real in Christ, especially as they were familiar with the role assigned to Moses and other views put forward by the Hellenists. The success of the preaching of Philip and his followers in Samaria confirms that the Samaritans were prepared to receive a Christian mission, particularly a mission carried out by *this* group.

In addition, the whole attitude of the Hellenists and of the Johannine circle must have led them to direct their attention beyond the narrower Jewish community and must have given them the idea of mission. We have seen[23] that a missionary interest can be traced throughout the Gospel of John: in ch. 10 about the good shepherd who must also bring other sheep who are not of this fold (v. 16); in 12.20ff., where the Greeks want to see Jesus and are told that the grain of wheat must first die in order to bring forth fruit, and in v. 32 of the same chapter, where Christ says that he will only draw *all* men to himself when he has been lifted up on the cross. We shall find this very idea in the second part of Jesus' discourse about the 'harvest' in Samaria, which we shall be discussing later: Jesus sows the seed at Jacob's well, but the harvest will be brought in by others. J. Bowman would also refer the passage mentioned above, about the other sheep (John 10.16), to the mission in Samaria and sees here an allusion to the two staffs in Ezek. 37, one for Judah and the other for Ephraim, the union of which symbolizes the union of Israel and Judah, who have 'one shepherd'.[24] This suggestion is worth considering.

Samaria, however, is especially significant because it is the starting point for *all* Christian mission. Here the preaching of the gospel for the first time goes out beyond the official Jewish sphere, even though there is a link between Samaria and Judaism. The mission to Samaria forms a natural transition towards the mission to the Gentiles.

Luke recognized the importance of the mission in Samaria. It could not escape him, since his aim was to make known the spread of the Gospel 'in Jerusalem and in all Judaea and *Samaria* and to the end of the earth' (Acts 1.8).[25] He understood that the proclamation of the gospel in Samaria was the decisive step towards the mission to the Gentiles. He also recorded the *initiative of the Hellenists* towards this mission, though he did not of course recognize or acknowledge their role or their significance. His tendency was to present the earliest community as a homogeneous group and he therefore attributed this great missionary undertaking to the *whole* church. Nevertheless, he has maintained the tradition according to which the evangelization of Samaria was begun by the Hellenists, whereas the Twelve only sent Peter and John there *after* the Samaritans had been converted and baptized (Acts 8.14ff.).[26] Luke names only one of the missionaries who came from Stephen's group: Philip. The others remain anonymous, although their work in this half-Jewish, half-Gentile land cannot be estimated too highly.

The Fourth Evangelist is the first to put their contribution in its proper light. As we shall see later, he is interested not only in the conversion of the Samaritans, like Luke, but also in these Hellenistic missionaries. He shares with Luke the knowledge of a common tradition about the role which they played. But unlike the author of Acts, he also gives express support to the activity of the Hellenists in Samaria.

The starting point is the meeting of Jesus with the woman of Samaria (ch. 4). In accordance with his characteristic perspective, the author reports an event in the life of Jesus and at the same time indicates its extension in the work performed by the exalted Christ in his church. What happens by Jacob's well gives him the opportunity in the first part of the discourse to communicate instruction about true worship which is important for the evangelization of Samaria, and in the second part, which is of interest to us now, to bring out the link between Jesus' meeting with the woman of Samaria and the future Christian mission in Samaria, which Jesus prophetically announces.

By making Jesus speak, the evangelist shows that he himself willed the mission in Samaria. This intention could be – and very probably was – disputed on the basis of Matt. 10.5 ('Do not go into the cities of Samaria').[27] Although the mission was only carried out after Jesus' death, it was *anticipated* in his lifetime: the people already hasten to Jesus from Sychar (John 4.30). Christ has 'sown', but the true harvest will only be gathered after his death.

It is, however, particularly interesting that the interest of the Gospel of John in the mission extends to the missionaries themselves, *to the Hellenists*. In the article in which I called attention for the first time to the link between the Hellenists and the Gospel of John,[28] I think I demonstrated that v. 38 is to be interpreted as a prophetic reference to what will really take place in Samaria, as recorded in Acts 8. This verse distinguishes the one who 'has sent the disciples into the harvest' (Christ, who did the sowing at an earlier time), and then two groups, first the *alloi*, those who 'have laboured', and then those who 'have entered into their labour'. My explanation is that the *alloi* who have 'laboured' in Samaria are none other than the Hellenists, who were the true missionaries of this area. Peter and John only went there later (Acts 8.14) on behalf of the disciples in Jerusalem: they 'entered into the labours of the *alloi*'.[29] In this instance the evangelist clearly does justice to these Hellenists, in contrast to an over-emphasis on the Petrine circle.[30] The reason for this must be that there was a special link between the Johannine circle and the 'Hellenists'.[31]

The mission to Samaria was evidently important to the two groups. This *event*, and probably also the *later* influence of converted Samaritans, brought out features which are particularly characteristic of Samaritan religion in the transmission of Stephen's speech (through the source used by Luke) and in the Gospel of John, in addition to those more general characteristics deriving from heterodox Judaism. At the same time, these latter features which were already present may have been increased by further doctrines peculiar to the Samaritans.

As we move on, then, to show as a further indication of the special link between the Johannine circle and the 'Hellenists' how the two groups derive *in the same way* from a heterodox Judaism, it is important to note two things: first their relationship to a *variety* of heterodox Jewish trends, and secondly the *predominance* of Samaritan characteristics.

3. *The common dependence of the two groups on heterodox Judaism*

We can detect the *twofold* relationship mentioned above in both Stephen's speech and the Gospel of John.

(a) Stephen's speech

A. F. J. Klijn thinks that many of the favourite ideas of the Qumran sect are to be found in Stephen's speech.[32] M. Simon stressed the affinity of the speech with the heretical Jewish Christianity of the Pseudo-Clementines.[33] Above all, however, the striking parallels between Stephen's speech in his own defence and the Samaritan religion have attracted the attention of scholars in most recent times. In an astonishing way, E. H. Plumptre had already anticipated the most recent theories about the Hellenists and the Samaritans almost a century ago.[34] Now, in a short study which is printed as an appendix to J. Munck's commentary on Acts,[35] Abram Spiro[36] points to a number of important doctrines of Samaritan religion, Samaritan traditions about the patriarchs, and even use of the Samaritan Pentateuch[37] and peculiarities of Samaritan style in Acts 7 which are so close to Stephen's speech that they compel him to conclude in connection with an old tradition handed down by the chronicler Abul Fath that Stephen was a Samaritan. M. H. Scharlemann does not go as far as this.[38] In his dissertation of 1968, however, he makes a careful comparison and follows Spiro and J. Bowman,[39] who himself refers to parallels, in assuming a fundamental Samaritan influence on Stephen, and he stresses the Samaritan character of the whole speech. To mention only a few points, there are: the interest in Joseph; the quotations from the Samaritan Pentateuch mentioned above; the significance of Shechem as the place where the patriarchs were buried, which was already stressed by Plumptre; the role of Joshua; the tabernacle;[40] the christology based on Deut. 18.15;[41] the designation of the temple as a 'place' (topos). Taken together, these parallels are impressive.[42] However, among the common features one should distinguish those which Stephen's speech also shares with other tendencies in non-conformist Judaism.[43] An article by R. Scroggs, which appeared in the same year as Scharlemann's study, has some points of contact.[44]

(b) The Gospel of John

As in Stephen's speech, we find in the Fourth Gospel a *multiplicity* of syncretistic influences which come together in heterodox Judaism; among them, Samaritan influence is particularly *prominent*. In the chapter above dealing with the milieu of the Gospel I mentioned numerous monographs written by a variety of scholars, and stressed that the Gospel shows notable parallels to heterodox Judaism and kindred phenomena which belong in the same sphere. I need not repeat that discussion here. At this point it is only necessary to lay particular emphasis on the Samaritan influence mentioned in that chapter, in the light of most recent work. It is important that J. Bowman,[45] a specialist in Samaritan questions, and W. A. Meeks,[46] in christology, have investigated the relationship between the Gospel of John and Samaritan doctrines. W. A. Meeks even comes to the conclusion that 'the Johannine church' must have included members who came from Samaritan groups.[47] At a later date, G. W. Buchanan goes even further.[48] He takes up my theory of the affinity between the Gospel of John and Acts 7. But in the Gospel his chief concern is not with the question of liturgy. He believes that in the Gospel he can find traces of a tacit polemic against the '*Ioudaioi*' as adversaries of the '*Israelitai*' (Samaritans).[49] Such a contrast is, he argues, only comprehensible coming from a Samaritan. Buchanan puts great stress on the terminology (also 'king of Israel' in 1.49 and 12.13 instead of 'Son of David'), which is part of the polemical arsenal of the Samaritans. So he does not hesitate to say that the author of the Gospel is a Samaritan converted to Christianity. This would explain the evangelist's interest in Samaria (ch. 4) and also the fact that in 8.48 the Johannine Christ rejects the taunt that he has a demon, while in the same passage he does not react to the other comment intended as a taunt, that he is a 'Samaritan'.

Buchanan has done valuable work in collecting these parallels, some of which are important, but they do not in themselves justify the conclusion which he draws from them. Instead of seeing the evangelist as a former Samaritan now converted to Christianity, which is indeed possible, we might do better to consider Bowman's theory that the Gospel was written for Samaritans. Be that as it may, here too, as in the question of the contact of Stephen's speech with Samaritan theology, I would recall that, following on from the preceding chapter, it is necessary not to limit oneself to Samaritan theology, relevant though that is, but also to consider the simultaneous influence of other groups and conceptions which belong to the same stream of heterodox Judaism: Qumran, the Mandaeans, the baptist movement, Jewish syncretism and gnostic Ebionitism.[50]

4. *The triangular relationship*

We have thus established on the one hand that Stephen's speech and the Gospel of John are related in the same way to heterodox Judaism and above all to that of Samaria, and on the other that Stephen's speech and the Gospel of John are still more closely related to each other. Accordingly, we have a *triangular relationship*, and it is in these terms that I would see the solution of the question about the special group around John which we raised at the beginning of this chapter. I would therefore suggest the following pattern:

Heterodox Judaism

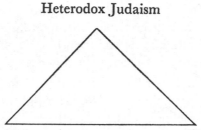

Stephen's speech   The Gospel of John

The apex of the triangle is represented by heterodox Judaism, in which Samaria plays a predominant role, but only *alongside* other analogous tendencies. It exercised simultaneous influence on Stephen's speech and the Gospel of John. The close relationship between the latter two which we have established *quite apart from* this twofold influence confirms that the background of the Gospel is to be sought in a Jewish environment analogous to that of the Jerusalem Hellenists (Stephen). Most scholars draw only one or two lines of the triangle, but it is only the connection of all *three* lines which indicates the strength of my argument for the connection between the Johannine group and the Hellenists.[51]

The situation is clarified by the fact that the opposition to the temple which is a common feature of almost all sectarian groups in Judaism is more radical in Acts 7 and the Gospel of John than in the Jewish heterodox movements, despite its contact with them. Because of a common belief in Christ, these two groups are closer to one another within the whole movement hostile to the temple than to the

Jewish sects. Whereas in Qumran, opposition to the temple is not *in principle* directed against the temple as such but only against the temple worship as carried on at that time in Jerusalem by a godless priesthood, and whereas Samaria also associates its worship with a particular place, Gerizim, despite its analogous opposition to the temple in *Jerusalem*, albeit from different motives, Stephen's speech rejects *any* particular localization of the divine presence apart from the portable sanctuary of the tabernacle. This is even more the case with the Gospel of John, which argues for neither Gerizim nor the temple in Jerusalem, but for worship in spirit and in truth.[52] The accord between Hellenists and the Gospel of John over against the less radical opposition of kindred heterodox Judaism is to be explained from their common belief in the presence of God in Christ. This conditions their negative attitude to *any* place of worship.

5.   *Further traces of the Johannine circle in the New Testament*

The hypothesis about the place of the Gospel of John within primitive Christianity which I present here seems to me to have both exegetical and historical foundations. It associates the 'Johannine circle' closely with the group of Jerusalem Hellenists. I would not go so far as to identify it unquestionably with this group, though the possibility is not to be ruled out. I would, however, in any case assign it to an analogous branch of Christianity, including these Hellenists, a branch of which we may find other indications elsewhere in the New Testament. Theologically it is distinct from both Jewish Christianity and Gentile Christianity. We have seen that the origin of *this* Palestinian Christianity from a more esoteric Judaism is different from that of the other trend, quantitatively more important, which led to the origin of the synoptic gospels.

As the group with which we are concerned is not isolated within earliest Christianity, the designation 'Johannine' is probably too narrow. Nevertheless, we shall keep to it in the following comments, as it does characterize the Gospel and Epistles of John in a special way. The *Johannine Epistles* certainly emerged from this group. Although it is probable that their author is not identical with the author of the Gospel,[53] the connection between the two must nevertheless have been very close, perhaps as close as that between the evangelist and the redactor, to whom indeed the composition of the Johannine Epistles is also often assigned. At any rate, he belongs to the same group.

The other New Testament book, the only one which seems to be rightly associated with the name of John, is the *Revelation of John*, as the name John is mentioned only here. This is harder to assign to the same circle, above all because its eschatology has a different orientation.[54] Nevertheless, there are reasons for indicating the affinity between certain images (e.g. Christ as 'lamb',[55] as 'shepherd', as 'living water') and concepts (like *marturia*) which are important for the two. The marked liturgical orientation of Revelation also brings it quite close to the Gospel of John. On the basis of the presupposition that liturgy is an anticipation of the end, many apocalyptic descriptions, as exegesis indicates, are taken from worship.[56] In the Gospel of John (ch. 4), the prophecy of the end time seems already to be realized: 'The hour is coming, and now is' (v. 23); in the heavenly city of Revelation there is no temple, as 'God and the lamb are the temple' (Rev. 21.22):[57] in both cases we have the important Johannine theme. It is worth noting that in the same chapter (v. 3) it is stated that the *skene* of God will dwell with men and that he will 'tabernacle' among them (cf. John 1.14: he 'tabernacled' among us). If the author belonged to the same circle – and this cannot be ruled out – we must at any rate assume that this circle held a variety of views, despite the features which it had in common. I John, which must certainly be assigned to it, also represents a more strongly futurist eschatology (I John 2.18; 3.2f.).[58]

It is very probable that we should think of the *Epistle to the Hebrews* as belonging to the Johannine group. This possibility must be considered very seriously from a number of points of view: there is a close connection in the evidently critical attitude of Hebrews to the temple and its more positive approach to the tabernacle (9.2; 9.11f.),[59] in its general interest in liturgy and also in its christological views. W. Manson already connected this book with Stephen's speech,[60] and in his great commentary on Hebrews, C. Spicq pointed out the many points of contact between the Gospel of John and Hebrews.[61] In view of the relationship between the Gospel of John and the Hellenists demonstrated above, this twofold relationship between Hebrews and the Hellenists and Hebrews and the Gospel of John seems to me to speak in favour of assigning Hebrews to the same group. A link between Hebrews and the Johannine circle is also established by the demonstration of many parallels to heterodox Judaism. Y. Yadin and H. Kosmala have already compared this writing, which is so strongly stamped with priestly ideas, to Qumran.[62] For our question, the affinity of Hebrews to Samaritan theology, put forward by E. A. Knox in 1927[63] and developed further since then,[64] is even more important.

The question whether traces of the Johannine circle may not also be found outside the New Testament will be raised in the next chapter.

6. Relations with the rest of earliest Christianity

Just as we cannot follow Scharlemann in describing Stephen as a 'solitary saint', isolating him from the 'Hellenists', so too we cannot follow E. Käsemann in detaching the whole Johannine circle with which we are concerned more or less entirely from the rest of earliest Christianity and assigning it to a 'corner'. Its members were probably aware of the difference which separated them from the church going back to the Twelve and also saw that their particular characteristics laid upon them the obligation of a special mission, namely to preserve, defend and hand on the distinctive tradition which they were sure had come down from Jesus himself. However, this awareness never led to direct polemic against the other Christians. Nevertheless, as a minority the group always found itself on the defensive and had to fight for its independence without in any way attacking the church founded on the Twelve. The ambivalent relationship which we shall establish in the Fourth Gospel between Peter, the representative of the rest of the earliest community, and the 'beloved disciple', reflects this twofold effort on the part of the Johannine circle very clearly: on the one hand it deliberately maintains its own independence, but on the other it is convinced of the need for mutual supplementation in the common interest.[65] The adoption of 'synoptic' tradition in addition to the special Johannine traditions points in the same direction.

On the other hand, the contrast should not be exaggerated, since the heterodox Judaism which inevitably dominated the Gospel of John by virtue of its origin was not completely lacking elsewhere in earliest Christianity.

We should not be surprised that the characteristic twofold attitude of the Gospel of John to the rest of the church again coincides with that of the Hellenists in Jerusalem. They too differ fundamentally from the Twelve, and therefore are treated differently by the Jews,[66] yet they too do not break off communion, although there are occasionally 'murmurings' against the Hebrews (Acts 6.1) and although the Jerusalem leaders of the community view them with mistrust and supervise their missionary work.[67]

In the end, of course, the unity of these two very different groups of disciples is grounded in Jesus himself. The question arises how far Jesus, who is usually associated in a one-sided way with only one of these groups, and is only presented in his relationship (albeit hostile) to official Judaism, is also in some way associated with heterodox Judaism, even if he transformed it and in many respects kept his distance from it. Did he also occasionally proclaim 'Johannine' doctrine as well as his synoptic preaching? We shall, however, only discuss this when we have considered the mysterious beloved disciple in connection with the complex problem of the authorship of the Gospel.

First of all, however, we must consider the further development of the Johannine circle in order to understand how it had to assert itself not only against the other trends in earliest Christianity but also against the heterodox Judaism from which it emerged, and how in the course of time it even had to engage in polemic against the latter.

VII

THE FURTHER DEVELOPMENT
OF THE JOHANNINE CIRCLE

I N THE TWO PREVIOUS CHAPTERS we have discussed above all
the derivation and the origin of Johannine Christianity within
earliest Christianity. However, the need to assume a development
of Johannine *traditions*[1] and to distinguish between the author and a
later editor or redactor(s) standing quite close to him means that
we must also raise the question of a further development of the
circle.

At an early stage the group was evidently extended by the in-
clusion of *converted Samaritans*. I stressed above[2] that even before the
mission to Samaria, the Hellenists and the Johannine circle contained
Samaritan as well as other heterodox Jewish elements, and that this
partly explained the rapid success of the evangelists in the area. At
the same time, it is also understandable that the Samaritans converted to Christ would for the most part have adopted the form of
Christianity represented by their *first* missionaries, the Hellenists,
which we might also term the Johannine form. The fact that these
Christian Samaritans would join the group not only increased its
numbers; the Samaritan influence on the Johannine circle which
was already present would now be substantially strengthened by the
new arrivals.[3]

The question of the further development of the circle must also be
raised in connection with the polemical tendencies which can be
demonstrated in the Gospel of John and in the Johannine Epistles.
We shall see that these writings were not composed when the group
was first formed and that the author of the Gospel only wrote it down

in old age, even if he is to be counted among the first founders of the group and is probably its most important representative. [4]

At the end of the previous chapter we saw that the Johannine circle was aware of being fundamentally different from the rest of Christianity, but was not divided from it and in opposition to it; there is thus no real polemic against 'synoptic' Christianity. We do however, find polemic allusions to trends in the marginal Judaism from which the circle arose, quite apart from remarks directed at official Judaism. In Johannine scholarship today there is a tendency to exaggerate the opposition between the Johannine group and the rest of earliest Christianity, making this a matter of open polemic; at the same time, however, there is a tendency to underestimate the scope of the real polemic against certain contemporary syncretistic movements contained in these writings. Alternatively, this is seen as only a late 'church' correction, and not as resistance offered within the original group itself.

Consequently we have today the tendency, represented by E. Käsemann, and mentioned several times already, to see the Gospel of John as a gnostic, docetic gospel. [5] The relationship of the Gospel with heterodox movements and their influence on it certainly does not exclude the possibility that the Gospel explicitly kept its distance from these trends, and although on the other hand polemic does not in principle exclude some affinity and influence, the anti-gnostic [6] and anti-docetic attitude implicitly demonstrable in the Gospel of John seems to me to be irreconcilable with the proposal that it should be regarded as a gnostic and docetic gospel.

Polemic against trends in marginal Judaism from converted Christians who came from that Judaism may have been hardly perceptible to begin with. Their common opposition to official Judaism probably meant that the link with more or less heterodox Judaism was not completely destroyed. As has already been said, the term 'the Jews' which we find so often in the Gospel of John could denote a common adversary in this sense. The continuation of some degree of solidarity, as well as the theological points of contact already mentioned, probably explains why the Hellenists had such speedy success in Samaria (Acts 8).

In time, however, this will have changed, above all when after the events of AD 70 the Johannine group settled in an area which contained the scattered remnants of most of these Jewish marginal groups and in which there would be open syncretism between these communities. This area was probably Transjordania, though Syria, too, should not be ruled out. In contrast to the Jewish Christianity of the Pseudo-Clementines, which fell victim to this syncretism, Johannine Christianity was strong enough to offer resistance.

In the next chapter we shall criticize a tradition which presupposes a journey by John the son of Zebedee, whom the tradition identifies as the author of the Gospel of John, to Asia Minor. Whatever else we may say of the tradition, it is at least correct that the Gospel was written in a setting which is not the area from which the group originated.

Now according to our earlier conclusions, the Johannine circle did not come into contact with heretical Judaism for the first time in these new surroundings, whether Transjordania or perhaps Syria. Rather, it found there all the tendencies *with which it had been familiar from the beginning*, and from some of which it took its origin, though these tendencies were now accentuated in syncretistic fashion. We must therefore suppose a *twofold* influence of heretical marginal Judaism on the Gospel of John: first that which naturally came with its very origin, and secondly that which began later, outside its place of origin, in marked syncretistic surroundings.[7] Today the chief and indeed the exclusive influence is thought to have taken place at the latter stage, since a derivation of the Johannine circle from apostolic times is rejected. In reality, this influence was probably less important because here the Johannine group was deliberately reacting in direct polemic against all the elements which were irreconcilable with its belief in Christ. The founders of the group had already assimilated at the time of their origin the common conceptions which could be reconciled with this faith, and which even served as a particularly appropriate means of expressing it.

The various trends discussed in the chapter about the milieu of the Gospel need, therefore, to be considered twice, first as a background at the time of the origin of the Johannine circle and then at a later stage, when they were subject to polemic.

In my article in the Bultmann Festschrift in 1954,[8] I thought that I had shown that the only explanation for the almost astonishing affinity between Qumran and the heretical Jewish Christianity of the Pseudo-Clementine *Kerygmata Petrou* was that the survivors of the Qumran sect, of whom we have no certain news after the Jewish war, moved to Transjordania and there were swallowed up in the Jewish-Christian heretical movements, which they in turn influenced strongly. In this way, the Johannine circle may once again have come into contact with Qumran ideas.[9]

It is clear that the heretical Jewish Christianity of the Pseudo-Clementines was in the same milieu as the Johannine group simply from the common front which both put up against the sect of the later *disciples of John the Baptist*, which was probably under syncretistic influence.[10] That the two groups attack the sect by completely different methods does not alter this fact in the slightest: the Pseudo-Clementines attack John the Baptist himself, and counter the chronological argument of John's disciples that Jesus was subordinate to the Baptist because he 'came later', by making John the Baptist, simply by virtue of his earlier origin, the principle of evil within the gnostic 'syzygies': Cain comes before Abel, Ishmael before Isaac, Esau before Jacob, Aaron before Moses, the Antichrist before Christ, the Baptist before Jesus. The Gospel of John, on the other hand, only attacks the false assessment of John the Baptist by the sect and not the Baptist himself. It accords him the high status of chief witness to the Logos made manifest in the flesh. The Logos himself is 'first' in an absolute way, as he was 'in the beginning' (1.15).

The Johannine group in part (especially those of its members who are relevant for the composition of the Gospel of John) emerged from the community of John the Baptist. Jesus himself and the first to follow him were former disciples of the Baptist (1.35ff.). If we were to draw a line from John the Baptist to Samaria on the basis of various texts,[11] there would be a further connection here. Be that as it may, we can understand the prologue itself to protest against the claims made by the sect for the Baptist: '*He* was not that light' (v. 8). In the narrative which follows immediately upon the prologue, John the Baptist himself gives particularly emphatic evidence against the claim: 'He confessed, he did not deny, but confessed, "I am not the Christ" ' (1.20). The evangelist also continues indirect polemic at a later stage (3.25ff.). Following W. Baldensperger[12] and W. Bauer,[13] Bultmann rightly stressed this polemic,[14] and then even went so far as to suppose that the prologue of the Gospel had been taken over by the author from the sect of the disciples of John: this earlier document had celebrated the Baptist.[15] This, however, seems to me to be doubtful. How could a Christian have taken over from the disciples of John, against whom he was fighting, a text whose statements were concerned with the ambassador whom these disciples revered? Still, be that as it may, I do agree with Bultmann that the relationship between John the Baptist's sect and the Johannine circle involved both influence *and* hostility: the first stage of their encounter will have resulted in the influence, whereas the second will have been marked by hostility. The sect of the Baptist must have been particularly influential in the area where the Johannine group settled; the sect will have been competition both for the Jewish Christians of the Pseudo-Clementines who moved there and for the Johannine group.

At this time the group may have had a further encounter with *Samaritans* who had not been converted, and who had earlier come under syncretistic influence in their homeland. The discussions between Peter and Simon Magus in the Pseudo-Clementines indicate that the gnosticizing Jewish Christians of the Pseudo-Clementines probably had to come to grips with the cult of Simon.[16]

It has already been stressed on a number of occasions that there is at least an indirect fight against *docetism* in the Gospel, as well as in the Johannine Epistles. We should probably follow the church fathers in seeing an anti-gnostic point in John 1.14.[17] Ignatius of Antioch bears witness that this heresy already emerged in a Jewish milieu, and not just in the sphere of the Greek diaspora, and that it has an explicit Jewish-Christian character.[18] There may well be traces of a docetic influence in the thought-world of Johannine Christianity, but its anti-docetic polemic does not allow us to follow Käsemann in seeing the Gospel itself as a docetic work.

Is it possible to trace the development of the Johannine circle further into the second century? In principle, I think that the question can be answered in the affirmative. However, the task is a difficult one because from a certain point in time onwards the group increasingly loses its special position and both ecclesiastically and theologically is taken up into the rest of Christianity. Still, with this proviso we can probably count Ignatius of Antioch as one of the successors to the circle, even if a historical link cannot be established. It would be tempting to look for further influence among other fathers, say in Irenaeus. However, the further we move from the beginnings, the more the Johannine type is mixed with synoptic and Pauline Christianity, especially as the rise of the New Testament canon has a cumulative effect.

Paradoxical though it may seem, the special characteristics of the original group were preserved in certain *gnostic* circles, albeit in a heretical form which ran contrary to the intention of their advocates. We should probably assume that while the general tendency was towards assimilation to the rest of Christianity, some groups succumbed to an opposite temptation, to remove themselves further by joining up with the gnostics. This may have developed further, as the Gospel of John exercised a certain attraction on the gnostics. There thus appeared an area common both to the heterodox Judaism from which the Johannine circle derived and to gnosticism.

This stage, however, would need further investigation, and with it we are far removed from the real subject of the present book.

To conclude: we follow most recent research in recognizing the effects of the encounter mentioned in this chapter between the Johannine circle and the syncretistic movement after AD 70. We see this encounter, however, in connection with a much earlier influence of such tendencies at the time when a group of disciples developed out of marginal Judaism.

We can only venture to answer the question whether the Johannine circle of disciples can be traced back to the life of Jesus, before Easter, when we have discussed the question of the authorship of the Gospel of John. In doing so, we shall keep in mind the results which have so far been achieved.

VIII

THE AUTHOR OF THE GOSPEL OF JOHN
AND THE JOHANNINE CIRCLE

IN THE PREVIOUS CHAPTERS we have spoken only in general terms about the author of the Gospel of John in connection with the literary character and the theological aim of the Gospel; now we shall seek to identify him. First the attempt had to be made to discover the chief characteristics of the Johannine circle, of whose existence there can be no doubt. However, the question of the identity of the individual author must be raised, especially as an examination of the Gospel suggested a strong literary and theological personality who must therefore be assigned an individual role within the group, because he took the initiative in writing a life of Jesus in its name. There are likely to be other reasons, too, for his predominance.

There is certainly no justification for the passion with which this complex question was discussed earlier, as though the value of the Gospel for Christian faith and Christian theology stood or fell with a solution. On the other hand, however, its significance should not be underestimated.

The discussion has been carried on almost *ad nauseam*. The reason why I am taking it up yet again in the present chapter is that I am convinced that the consequences of the most recent work on the background of the Gospel and the derivation and character of the Johannine circle have not yet been brought to bear on all the aspects of the problem of authorship. The discussion of the question of the authorship of the Gospel has failed, so to speak, to keep pace with more recent research into its *environment*. What seems to me to be the place of the Johannine circle in earliest Christianity appears to shed new light on this old problem.

1.   *The problem*

Right at the start we once again come up against the difficulty which faced us in connection with a discussion of the other questions relating to the Gospel. At this point, however, it becomes particularly acute. Of which author are we speaking? Of the author of the original Gospel? Of the final redactor? Of intermediary redactors? Of the author of a particularly important source? Of a man revered in the Johannine circle who could have been regarded by tradition as the author of the Gospel, because his testimony stood *behind* the real author, although he himself had not composed the Gospel?

I mention this last possibility because two substantial commentaries, by R. E. Brown and R. Schnackenburg, and the important work of the Belgian theologian F. M. Braun,[1] all put it forward as a theory, and are not the first to do so.[2] They distinguish the author of the Gospel from the apostle John, the son of Zebedee: the latter is only in the background, so to speak as an authority. Although they all put forward the same theory, the three Catholic scholars differ slightly in the details of their proposals: for F. M. Braun the writer of the Gospel was only a secretary, while the authority was responsible for its conception, whereas according to R. E. Brown and R. Schnackenburg the role of the writer of the Gospel and his literary and theological independence should be put much higher.

If we begin from the pattern which I proposed in the chapter on the literary unity of the Gospel:[3] oral tradition (parts of which were perhaps also fixed in writing); written Gospel, which was composed by a man who was responsible for the whole outline and the basic theological aim; and a complete revision of the whole work by a redactor (or group of redactors), we shall be concerned in this chapter with the man who wrote the basic work. We shall call him the evangelist. In connection with this we must point out from the start that the role of the authority assumed by R. E. Brown and Schnackenburg, which is hazy and hard to visualize, hardly allows us to assign to this figure so original a conception of the aim and the literary and theological perspective of the Gospel.[4] We shall only be

able to give a final answer to the question whether there is nevertheless also an 'authority' behind the evangelist when we come to the
end of this chapter, having investigated the external and internal
evidence about authorship.

The *external* evidence asserts the identity of the evangelist with the
apostle John; the *internal* evidence contained in the closing verses
of ch. 21 identifies him with an anonymous eyewitness: according
to this, the Gospel was written by the 'beloved disciple', who
is mentioned on several occasions from the passion narrative
on.

From the beginning, then, we must distinguish between two
questions which are all too often confused: Is the author (or according to the hypotheses mentioned above, the authority) identical with
the apostle John? Is the author (or the authority) an eyewitness?
The first question begins from external evidence and the second from
internal evidence; the second does not necessarily imply the first, as
the name of the eyewitness is never mentioned explicitly in the
Gospel.

In addition to the external and the internal evidence there is a
third solution, which has only been put forward by critical scholarship (and in fact by the majority of modern scholars): according to
this, neither the apostle John nor an eyewitness would be involved.
This means that both the external and the internal evidence in this
case are in dispute. We shall therefore make a brief critical examination of the evidence which is so often investigated so thoroughly in
Introductions to the New Testament. We shall begin with the most
important internal evidence. In contrast to the usual treatment in
Introductions, however, we shall first attempt to describe the author
in terms of *the content of the whole Gospel*, leaving out those passages
which refer to the anonymous disciple who in 21.24 is identified
with the author. Only when we have obtained a *general* picture of the
author from the Gospel as a whole will we compare this with the
direct external and internal evidence. The attempt to gain a picture
of the author from the general character of the Gospel follows on
directly from the results of the previous chapter.

2. *General characteristics of the author according to the*
content of the Gospel, apart from the passages relating
to the unnamed (beloved) disciple

As we have seen, the farewell discourses allow us to guess at the significance of the call to be an evangelist which the author is conscious of having been given. He knows himself to be inspired by the Paraclete, who 'teaches him all things and brings to his remembrance all that Jesus has said to him' (John 14.26). As I have stressed on a number of occasions, the Greek word for 'call to remembrance' in John refers not only to the recollection of a material event or a saying spoken by Jesus on a particular occasion, but also to the deeper understanding of them.[5] The disciples are promised a remembrance in this sense. The author certainly includes his own activity as an evangelist in the realization of this recollection when in 16.12 he records as a saying of Jesus, 'I have yet many things to say to you, but you cannot bear them now. When the Spirit of truth comes, he will guide you into all the truth.' By virtue of this conviction he feels himself called to set the events in the particular theological perspective of which we have spoken. This perspective presupposes that he is writing some time after the death of Jesus and that he is preoccupied with the organization of the community and its problems, especially those of liturgy and mission.

The whole content of the Gospel indicates that the author comes from a Jewish circle which differs from mainstream Judaism and has been shaped by alien influences. He regards the temple cult as finished, since from now on the divine presence is bound up with the person of Christ in his incarnation and with worship 'in spirit and in truth'.

He is particularly interested in John the Baptist and is concerned to combat the sect which appeals to him by making his function independent of that of Jesus. For a disciple of Jesus, this is no longer possible. He accords great significance to the mission in Samaria and to those who introduced the gospel there, the 'Hellenists' of Jerusalem.

The special interest in Judaea indicated by the selection of narratives suggests that he comes from Judaea.[6] At many points the passion narrative, which also belongs there, seems to have greater historical value than that of the synoptic gospels.

The Twelve play hardly any part in the Gospel as a group (they are only mentioned once, in 6.70). On the other hand, other intimate disciples of Jesus like Nathanael and Lazarus appear at decisive points. From this we may probably conclude that the evangelist himself was not one of the Twelve. In addition to the common tradition, he has special recollections at his disposal which go back to a different milieu from that of the Galilean fishermen. People also emerge in the Gospel who belong to another social stratum.

The author gives evidence of a high degree of education. This is indicated by his theological assessment of the life of Jesus, from which further lines are developed. He has taken over the mode of thought and certain thought-forms of the Judaism influenced by Hellenism from which he emerged.

His intensive concern to provide a link between the incarnate Jesus and the church, and his special traditions, above all about the teaching of Jesus, indicate that he belongs to a group, indeed even to a community, which cherishes a Christianity different from that of the synoptics and Paul, despite the common Christian heritage. By his way of describing the life of Jesus he means to indicate that this type of Christianity *also goes back to the incarnate Jesus*. Nevertheless, as has been said, the author and his fellow-believers do not wish to be a kind of sect. His universalism and his care for the *unity* of the church, his use of traditions which he has in common with the synoptics in addition to the traditions which are independent of them, confirm that he is maintaining a relationship with the church as a whole, despite his awareness of the lofty mission of his group and his Gospel.

The Gospel gives us no way of discovering the name of its author.

These, then, are the elements which we must now compare, first with the external evidence and then with the internal evidence of those passages in the Gospel which speak of the anonymous disciple.

3.   *The external evidence*

We shall not dwell on the detailed discussions of external evidence which can be read in any Introduction to the New Testament, but limit ourselves to a number of points which are relevant here.

Tradition claims to know the name of the author about which the Gospel itself is silent: he is said to have been the apostle John, the son of Zebedee. This tradition is, however, late, and does not go back beyond the end of the second century where Irenaeus writes for the first time: 'John the disciple of the Lord, who also reclined on his bosom, published his Gospel when he was living in Ephesus' (*Adv. haer.* III, 1, 2). At another point he says that John lived there in the time of Trajan (*Adv. haer.* III, 3, 4); as he calls him here 'witness to the tradition of the apostles', he obviously means John the son of Zebedee, although in the passage mentioned first he only calls him 'disciple of the Lord'. Irenaeus claims to have known presbyters, and especially Polycarp, who themselves knew John, but this John is not described in more detail. He is included among those who saw the Lord.[7] However, although the Muratorian canon from Rome supports this testimony of Irenaeus, neither witness enables us to put an early date to the tradition. Bishop Polycrates (towards 190) mentions the tomb at Ephesus of 'John, who was a priest and reclined on the bosom of the Lord', but this does not take us any further.

Attempts have been made to dispute the evidence of Irenaeus so to speak *a priori* by asserting that John the son of Zebedee suffered martyrdom at the same time as his brother James, that is in 44, leaving no time for him to have composed the Gospel. However, on the one hand this extremely uncertain dating rests on quite late texts, one from the fifth and the other from the ninth century, from authors who will have read the detail about the martyrdom of John in Papias, whereas on the other hand the chief argument which the assertion is meant to support is very problematical. It is said that the saying in Mark 10.39, in which Jesus prophesies a martyr's death for *both* sons of Zebedee at the same time, is a '*vaticinium ex eventu*', that is, a prophecy put on the lips of Jesus after the two sons had already been killed, and that as we know that James was martyred in 44 (Acts 12.1), this date can also be applied to the death of his brother John on the basis of Mark 10.39. Without the great academic authority of Eduard Schwartz, who put forward this theory,[8] it would probably never have been taken as seriously as in fact has been the case.

Quite apart from the questionable nature of this argument, however, Irenaeus' testimony about the composition of the Gospel by

John, one of the sons of Zebedee whom Jesus had named 'sons of thunder', remains very problematical. It can hardly be reconciled with the general characterization of the author which we have arrived at through an examination of the content of the Gospel, and in particular it does not tally with the supposition that the author of the Gospel came from Judaea, since the sons of Zebedee were Galileans. Other problematical features are the fact that he belonged to a group of disciples which appears different from that of the Twelve and had control of independent traditions; the influence of a heterodox Palestinian Judaism,[9] the author's relatively high standard of education and his contact with men from other social circles. One might also argue that if the epithet 'sons of thunder' is meant to refer to the temperament of the two brothers (which is, of course, uncertain), it does not accord with the evangelist's introvert character.

The same difficulties also arise if we follow the suggestion that the apostle John was only an authority and not the real author of the Gospel.[10] How could one assume that the evangelist based his work on the testimony of a disciple who was so completely different from his own circle? If he himself was not one of the Twelve, it is hardly conceivable that he might have appealed to one of the Twelve. This applies not only to his theological orientation but also to his use of independent special traditions. We shall have to ask the same question later when we compare the internal evidence about the 'beloved disciple' with the picture which we have constructed from the general character of the Gospel.

First of all, however, we must make a comparison with another piece of external evidence about the author of the Gospel, that of Papias (according to Eusebius, *HE* III, 39, 3). In a list of the people from whom he made enquiries he twice mentions a John, first among the 'elders', together with the apostles, who are also described as 'disciples of the Lord' (here John appears between James and Matthew), and then with Aristion. This second John is also designated an 'elder' (*presbyteros*), and he and Aristion are *also* named 'disciples of the Lord', at any rate in the text as we have it. Nevertheless, there is certainly a distinction here between two Johns. However, the endless discussions of the exegetical problems thrown up by this text (and for them I would refer the reader to an Introduction to the New Testament) only show that its significance for the question at issue has been exaggerated. In this case it is doubtless the authority of Harnack which has contributed so greatly to the arguments which have been based on this testimony and repeated in numerous variant forms.[11]

The hypothesis of a confusion between the apostle John and a 'presbyter' John which is based on this text doubtless owes its popularity to the fact that at least an attempt is made to associate the name 'John' with the Gospel, even if this is not the John meant by Irenaeus. Harnack himself believed that the apostle John was a kind of 'authority', whereas the author was the presbyter 'John'. Other variants of the theory eliminate the apostle John entirely in favour of the 'presbyter John'.[12] All of them point out that Dionysius of Alexandria (c. 265) mentions the presence of two 'tombs of John' in Ephesus and therefore knows of two Johns, one of whom is thought to have been the author of Revelation. Finally, theories relating to the presbyter John draw on the designation 'elder' (presbyteros) which is adopted by the author of II and III John, without of course adding the name John.

However, if we are also to assume the existence of a presbyter John, first we not only know nothing about him, but we do not even have an ancient text which clearly asserts that the Gospel was written by him. In these circumstances it is very doubtful whether he should be identified with the author. We may raise the same question about this hypothesis as about the tradition that the apostle John was the author: does it fit with the conclusions about authorship which may be drawn from the content of the Gospel? In this context its one advantage would seem to be that it puts the evangelist outside the group of the Twelve. We cannot tell whether the other characteristics fit the hypothetical 'presbyter John', since, as has been said, we know nothing about him.

We must therefore move on to those passages which speak of an anonymous disciple and suggest that the author is giving *direct* evidence about himself. We shall compare them, too, with the general characteristics which we have inferred from the rest of the Gospel apart from these passages.

4. *The internal testimony of the Gospel to the anonymous disciple*

First of all we shall look at the passages about 'the disciple whom Jesus loved', and then at the two others in which an unnamed disciple appears, though he is not of course described in the same way. The so-called 'beloved disciple' is mentioned for the first time in 13.23ff. At the last supper he reclines on Jesus' breast. Peter turns to him to discover Jesus' view of the identity of his betrayer. In 19.26 he stands beneath the cross and Jesus entrusts his mother to him. In 20.2ff. he and Peter are told by Mary Magdalene that the tomb is empty and the two then immediately run there. Peter is the first to arrive, then the beloved disciple: the latter enters, 'sees and believes' (v. 8). The beloved disciple appears twice in ch. 21, which is probably an addition: first of all in v. 7, where he is in a boat on Lake Tiberias and recognizes the risen Lord, then in vv. 20–24. Here he is following Peter when the latter turns round and, on seeing him, asks Jesus about the beloved disciple's destiny. Jesus replies: 'If it is my will that he remain until I come, what is that to you? Follow me.' The redactor adds that this saying of Jesus was made known among the disciples and was interpreted to mean that 'this disciple would not die'. But the redactor explicitly corrects what he regards as a false interpretation by repeating the actual words of Jesus' saying and stresses that Jesus did not say that the beloved disciple would not die. It is quite clear that here the redactor feels obliged to make this correction because the disciple *had* in fact meanwhile died, probably a short time beforehand. The next verse, v. 24, which we have already mentioned, explicitly says that this was the disciple 'who is bearing witness to these things, and who has written these things'. This is clearly a final explanation given by the redactor about the author of chs. 1–20.

(a) *Is the beloved disciple identical with the two anonymous figures in 1.35ff. and 18.15ff?*

To the passages already listed we must add two more, in which an anonymous disciple appears, though here he is not described as the disciple whom Jesus loved. The first is in 1.35ff. Two disciples of John the Baptist follow Jesus and ask him where he lives. One is named, Andrew, the brother of Simon Peter (who appears in v. 41).

The other is not named. Why this strange silence? The same question arises in the second passage, 18.15ff. Peter and 'another disciple' whose name is not given follow Jesus after his arrest. As the anonymous disciple is known to the high priest, he takes Peter into the palace.

Two considerations make it very probable that we should identify the unnamed disciple in these two passages with the 'beloved disciple'. First, the two disciples have in common the fact that they are given no name. Even here we should suppose that in *both* cases this silence suggests some relationship with the author. It is difficult to see any other reason. We have seen that in 21.24 the beloved disciple is said to be identical with the author, an assertion which we must now examine from other standpoints.

The second reason why the two passages about the anonymous disciple should be taken with those which speak of the beloved disciple is their context. In both passages, as in those about the beloved disciple, *the disciple is set alongside Peter*, and in the second passage we have the same theme: there is no polemic against Peter, but he nevertheless occupies an inferior position to that of the beloved disciple.

(b) Are the passages about the beloved disciple a later insertion?

Before we ask whether the evidence of the Gospel itself allows us to speak more precisely about this mysterious disciple, we must examine another theory which has frequently been put forward. This is that the passages about the beloved disciple in the Gospel have been inserted by the redactor who wrote ch. 21 with its closing verses and on the occasion of the 'spear thrust' (19.35) perhaps also added the note about the authenticity of the testimony of the one 'who saw it'. If we examine the passages about the beloved disciple *in the light of the general theological direction of the Gospel*, they at any rate fit this very well. The almost constant confrontation between Peter and the beloved disciple which presents the two disciples as supplementing each other, while at the same time giving the beloved disciple a certain preference, entirely accords with the fact that the *whole* Gospel, quite apart from the passages mentioned, testifies to a theology and traditions different from those of the Twelve: the traditions of the Twelve stand behind the *synoptic* tradition and Peter appears there as spokesman. On the other hand, the fact that, outside John 21, the beloved disciple only appears in narratives set in Judaea corresponds with the special interest of the *whole* Gospel in Judaea.

Both 1.35ff. and 18.15ff. similarly presuppose a situation characteristic of the *whole* Gospel: the first, which presents the unnamed disciple as a former disciple of John the Baptist, explains the explicit interest of the Gospel in the Baptist's sect; the second, which mentions his acquaintance with the high priest, accords with the observation that according to the *whole* Gospel the author knows men who come from other social circles.

We may also ask whether the way in which the author of ch. 21 introduces the beloved disciple in v. 20 as the one who reclined on Jesus' breast at the last supper does not become more understandable if it refers to a passage in the Gospel as this redactor had it before him, instead of supposing that he himself first inserted the passage in 13.23.

Nevertheless, the theory that all the passages about the beloved disciple were additions by the redactor probably has some grain of truth. If the evangelist introduced himself into the narrative in the person of this disciple, it is hard to understand how he could describe himself as 'the one whom Jesus loved'. We have seen that in 18.25 the anonymous disciple is simply called 'another disciple'.[13] In 20.2 the word 'another', Greek *allos*, is combined with the designation 'the one whom Jesus loved'. These two passages make it seem very plausible that all the passages relating to this disciple originally called him *'another disciple'* and that it was the redactor who first added the words 'the one whom Jesus loved'.[14] It may be fortuitous that he left out this addition in 18.15. The disciple may not yet have the designation in 1.37ff. because this is his first meeting with Jesus: the special favour shown to him by Jesus would have become evident only during Jesus' last stay in Jerusalem, and particularly at the last supper.

Be this as it may, it seems to me unnecessary and indeed improbable to assume that the passages about the beloved disciple are additions made by the redactor. But in that case, who is the mysterious anonymous disciple of whom the Gospel speaks? This question leads us to examine the various explanations put forward to solve the riddle.

(c) Attempts at identification

One radical solution which makes all attempts at historical identification superfluous from the start is to consider the disciple not to be a historical personality at all, but a symbolic ideal figure. The difficulty which arises when one tries to identify him directly with one of the disciples known from the synoptic gospels has contributed to the success of this hypothesis. A. Jülicher, A. Loisy, M. Goguel and others already regarded the beloved disciple as a symbol of the *ideal* disciple, with no historical reality. Others saw him as the personification of a particular early Christian group: Bultmann as a symbol of Hellenistic Christianity (in Bultmann's understanding) providing a contrast to the Jewish Christianity represented by the mother of Jesus and Peter; A. Kragerud as a symbol of prophetic Christianity in contrast to institutional Christianity. The 'collective' interpretation of the disciple was made with slight differences, depending on the way in which the character of the Johannine group was defined.

Although I myself have strongly stressed the character of the Johannine church as a community in all the previous chapters, I do not believe that a solution to the riddle is to be found in the collective explanations. Nevertheless, they too contain a grain of truth. We have seen that throughout the Gospel, persons and events in the narratives about the life of Jesus have a 'typical' significance as they simultaneously point to the situation in the church. In the chapters on the purpose and historical value of the Gospel I have also stressed that the author means to show the close *connection* between history and its theological value for the church: a historical event concerns at the same time both the life of the incarnate Jesus and its prolongation in the life of the church. The evangelist never *invents* an event or a person for allegorical ends. *For him* the historical character of events is a quite indispensable and fundamental element of his thesis. Thus it is indeed the case that the 'beloved disciple' represents his community, his particular group which has emerged from nonconformist Judaism, just as Peter, with whom he is contrasted, 'represents' the Christianity which grew out of official Judaism. But to conclude from this that the beloved disciple is an ideal figure and never existed is irreconcilable with the purpose of the Gospel as we have defined it.

Besides, the argument which has led to this theory must logically lead to the absurd conclusion that Peter, *who is the regular counterpart of the beloved disciple*, is also only an 'ideal figure'. Moreover, 21.20–24, in which the redactor gives a very precise explanation about the beloved disciple, would be incomprehensible if it did not refer to a real individual person. The way in which the redactor speaks of this disciple there, the official denial which he feels obliged to make of the interpretation of a saying of Jesus which relates to the disciple as though it meant 'this disciple will not die', are such clear indications of a specific historical situation that any attempt to conceal the fact or to explain it away must be regarded as impossible. The redactor is evidently correcting the interpretation because the beloved disciple has meanwhile *died*. This cannot relate to an ideal figure.

In due course we shall raise the question whether the disciple really wrote the Gospel himself or whether he is only the authority behind the author at a later stage. For the moment, I am merely concerned to affirm that the redactor who wrote ch. 21 connects the origin of the Gospel with a *specific* disciple and that the rest of the passages about the disciple also suggest this connection to the reader, no matter how he may imagine it.

Does internal evidence allow us to guess at the *name* of this disciple? We have seen that Irenaeus' assertion that the author was the apostle John can hardly be reconciled with the general evidence of the Gospel. This must now also be said specifically of the passages about the unnamed disciple. Not one of them contains even an indirect reference to the apostle John. John 1.41, which is often used to support the Irenaeus tradition, does not in fact make any allusion at all to the apostle John.

To come nearer to the solution we must first of all rid ourselves of the expectation that the disciple must be sought among the Twelve.[15] We should not begin from the synoptic tradition to solve this Johannine problem. Nothing in the Johannine narrative of the last supper at which the beloved disciple reclined on Jesus' breast suggests that only the Twelve were present.[16] We have seen that the Twelve do not play any essential role anywhere in the Fourth Gospel (they appear only once, in 6.70), and that on the contrary we find other intimate disciples like Nathanael and Lazarus close to Jesus. Above all, however, the passages about the unnamed disciple focus on a contrast between him and Peter: although there is no polemic, this almost suggests competition between the two. This contrast indicates that the disciple was not one of the Twelve, but the representative of a particular group of disciples, just as Peter is a representative of the Twelve.

Chapter 21 in particular seems to me virtually to exclude the possibility that the redactor who wrote it was thinking of John the son of Zebedee in his allusions to the beloved disciple. John 21.2 enumerates the disciples who were witnesses to the miraculous catch made when the risen Jesus appeared by Lake Tiberias. *Apart from* Peter, Thomas, Nathanael and the *two sons of Zebedee*, two other (Greek *alloi*) anonymous disciples were present. In v. 7 the beloved disciple speaks to Peter. That he is one of the two sons of Zebedee mentioned in v. 2 is a most improbable hypothesis,[17] for how could the redactor have broken in v. 2 the silence which he observes in v. 7 and everywhere else? It is much more probable that the anonymous beloved disciple of v. 7 is one of the two similarly anonymous disciples who in v. 2 are mentioned as *alloi*. This is the expression used by the Fourth Gospel where it speaks of the beloved disciple.[18] Just as Nathanael, who appears in the list in 21.2, does not belong to the Twelve, so the two *alloi* must also be sought outside the Twelve: one of them is identical with the beloved disciple, whereas the other very probably belongs to the group which stands behind the Gospel. As v. 24 identifies the disciple with the author, it would also be necessary to repeat here all the arguments by which I have shown that it is impossible to reconcile the picture of the author derived from the content of the Gospel with what we know of John the son of Zebedee.[19]

But is it possible to find a *name* for the author if he is to be sought *outside the group of Twelve*? An attempt has been made. Two names in particular have been suggested, first that of *John Mark*.[20] It must be conceded that this hypothesis has some support in the fact that according to Acts 12.12, John Mark had a house in Jerusalem and that as a cousin of Barnabas the Levite (Col. 4.10; Acts 4.36) he was connected with the priestly class, which would fit John 18.15.[21]

Finally, the traditional claim that the Gospel was written by the apostle John could be explained by a confusion between this John and John Mark. It is, however, difficult to see these arguments as indicating more than a possibility.

The same is true of another hypothesis, which can also be supported by a number of arguments which are well worth considering: this hypothesis identifies the beloved disciple with *Lazarus*. He too is a disciple from Judah who was not one of the Twelve. In particular, he is the only one of whom it is said that Jesus loved him (11.3, 5, 36). Moreover, the beloved disciple only appears after the narrative about the raising of Lazarus, and this story occupies a central position within the Gospel. The saying which circulated in the earliest community, that 'this disciple will not die' (21.23), could be explained particularly well if it referred to Lazarus. The hypothesis is an old one and has been taken up and varied at different times, particularly by F. V. Filson and K. A. Eckhardt.[22] The latter also identifies Lazarus with the apostle John: he was given the name Lazarus after his resurrection. The fact that the same disciple is mentioned by name in ch. 11 whereas elsewhere he remains anonymous seems to me to present a serious difficulty for this hypothesis, but it cannot be ruled out altogether.[23]

It is, however, probably superfluous to want to give the great anonymous figure a name and identify him with one of the disciples mentioned in the New Testament.[24] According to what we have noted so far, he belonged to a special group which for want of a better name we have called 'Johannine'. As this group had its place more on the edge of the Christianity which went back to the Twelve and is represented by the synoptic tradition, it is not surprising that the names of its members were less well known. We do not know the names of most of the Hellenist missionaries from Jerusalem mentioned in Acts, either.[25]

However, the very fact that the beloved disciple is anonymous does suggest that he was a historical figure. The apocryphal gospels tend to connect their legendary accounts with a known disciple rather than with an anonymous person.

We must therefore be content with *remaining in ignorance about the name of this beloved disciple.* However, what the Gospel tells us about him allows us to draw quite a specific picture of him. We shall sum up its main features here once again. As he only appears in scenes which take place in Judaea, at the beginning and the end of the Gospel, we must assume that he comes from this region and that Jesus met him in Judaea. He is a former disciple of John the Baptist. He began to follow Jesus in Judaea when *Jesus himself was in close proximity to the Baptist.* He shared the life of his master during Jesus' last stay in Jerusalem. He was known to the high priest. His connection with Jesus was different from that of Peter, the representative of the Twelve. Although he does not dissociate himself directly from Peter, he seems to demonstrate his faithfulness to Jesus in another way: less by activity than by a deepening of faith. This particular aspect of his personality also emerges after the death of Jesus. Without taking a stand against Peter, he goes his own way. The fact that the final redactor published or completed his work and made a declaration about it in the first person plural ('we know') seems to indicate that the disciple collected a whole group of followers about himself.

(d) Is the disciple identical with the author?

We must now ask whether this picture of the beloved disciple corresponds with the picture that we have sketched out at the beginning of this chapter[26] of the author of the Gospel on the basis of its *content* alone, *quite independently of the passages which concern the beloved disciple.* In other words, is the claim of the redactor in 21.24, 'This is the disciple who has written these things', confirmed by the content of the Gospel as a whole? When we put the same question about the tradition relating to John the son of Zebedee we were forced to give a negative answer on the basis of a comparison between what we know about the apostle John and what the Gospel as a whole tells us of its author. On the other hand, all the distinctive characteristics of the beloved disciple which we have discovered correspond with the picture that we constructed from the content of the Gospel alone. We have already demonstrated this in part in another context,[27] in dealing with the question of the place of the passages about the beloved disciple in the original Gospel. We need not therefore repeat all the points here, and simply limit ourselves to those which show

how the passages about the beloved disciple *supplement* and do not contradict the picture of the author which we obtained by indirect means.

John 1.35ff. expressly states that the anonymous figure was once a disciple of John the Baptist. We can see from this how the author came to find his place in marginal Judaism; at the same time, we can well understand the above-mentioned polemic against the sect which appealed to John the Baptist. The presupposition in 18.15 that the beloved disciple was acquainted with the high priest sheds light on his relationship to people from a different social status from most of those named in the synoptic gospels. The great interest of the Gospel in the question of the temple, in Jewish feasts and in ritual customs may also be connected with this. We should not forget that the very narratives in which the anonymous disciple makes an appearance, like the account of the first meeting with Jesus in Judaea, near to the work of John the Baptist, and then especially the passion narrative, are those in which a good historical nucleus can be discovered. Finally, the note of the redactor in 21.23ff., about the disciple of whom it was said 'he will not die', suggests that he reached a considerable age and survived all other eyewitnesses.[28] This fits very well with the detached consideration of the life of Jesus and the special perspective of which we have spoken, in which only a man who had lived a long life could set events.[29]

All this may be said in favour of the correctness of the redactor's note that the beloved disciple was the author of the Gospel. However, a problem of a special kind now arises in connection with the identification of the author with the beloved disciple. Can the evangelist have been an eyewitness? Various difficulties arise here: as has been mentioned above, the Gospel contains not only good and historically valuable traditions or reminiscences but also evidently later elements which indicate a lengthy and secondary stage of development in the tradition, which is hard to reconcile with eyewitnesses; the high theology of Jesus' doctrine in the Gospel of John is very different from the 'simpler' preaching of the kingdom of God in the synoptic gospels. Then there is the psychological difficulty: can an eyewitness, who shared Jesus' life at a particular point, speak as the author does of the exalted Christ who is united with God and – if he himself added the prologue to the Gospel – of the Christ Logos who took part in creation?

We have already remarked above that the first-mentioned difficulty can be resolved by a reference to the work of the redactor: to him may be attributed the insertion of later elements which are less reliable in comparison with those in the synoptic gospels. However, not *all* the later features can be explained in this way. There are a large number of narratives, some which take place in Galilee and some in Judaea, which must come from the evangelist and cannot derive from the redactor, and whose historicity still seems less satisfactorily guaranteed than the others. At this point we should remember that the claim that the author is an eyewitness cannot mean that he is an eyewitness of all the narratives which he reports; for happenings about which he had no memories of his own he perhaps even used sources accessible in his circle, some of which may already have undergone a lengthy development.[30] It has been objected that an eyewitness does not take refuge in sources. But this is an inadmissible *a priori* argument. The beloved disciple is less of an eyewitness of the *whole* public ministry of Jesus because he comes from Judaea and belongs to a group which is not that of the Twelve. *These* disciples certainly did not follow Jesus everywhere. If we are writing the biography of a dead friend with whom we worked for a certain period of his life, we too look for other people's accounts about other periods of his life.

I would even assume that the author of the Gospel of John was an eyewitness of only a limited number of the events which he records. For the others he used tradition. The fact that we must judge some of these traditions of less value from a historical point of view does not mean that the author shared our judgment. I may recall here what was said above about the purpose of the Gospel and the relationship between theology and history in its thought.[31] So I see no obstacle here to prevent us from identifying the disciple with the author.

The difference between the profound Johannine theology and Jesus' simple proclamation of the kingdom of God in the synoptic gospels is used as a particularly emphatic argument against the possibility that the author of the Gospel was an eyewitness. This argument is based on two presuppositions: first, that the eyewitness can only have been an 'unlearned Galilean fisherman', and secondly that Jesus can only have preached in the form known to us in the synoptic gospels.

To begin with the first point: the whole of the present work should have demonstrated that both the author of the Gospel and those among whom he worked emerged from a heterodox Judaism which was already in existence at the time of Jesus, and which contained ideas drawn from Hellenistic syncretism as well as apocalyptic doctrines. I cannot see why representatives of this kind of Judaism should not have attached themselves to Jesus. Indeed, it would be astonishing if such Jews *especially* had not felt drawn to him.

I shall be discussing the second question, whether we might attribute a different kind of preaching to Jesus from that found in the synoptic gospels, in the next chapter. At this point, however, I should like to bring up a number of points in connection with a consideration of the difficulties which arise if we assume that the author was an eyewitness. Is it beyond the realms of possibility that Jesus himself had connections with that form of heterodox Judaism without necessarily belonging to it? Does the frequent use of the title 'Son of Man' not point in this direction?[32] I would also recall a Q saying from Matt. 11.27; Luke 10.22, which is often cited to suggest that on occasion Jesus could speak in a different way: 'No one knows the Son except the Father, and no one knows the Father except the Son. . . .' This has been felt to be an 'alien' Johannine element within the synoptic preaching, but it is nevertheless an element of the old Q source. The authenticity of the saying has often been disputed, but the reasons given are not compelling, and I would refer here to a remark made by Albert Schweitzer in his *Quest of the Historical Jesus*: 'But the powerful hymn in Matt. 11.25–27 makes one think: v. 27 may have been spoken from an awareness of pre-existence.'[33] Unless we eliminate all the sayings about Jesus' awareness of himself in the synoptic gospels as 'community formations', we shall find there other traces of a proclamation which does not fit into too simplified a pattern of 'simple' preaching.

Of course, Jesus would hear nothing of secret doctrines like those in the heterodox sects, of which the strict Qumran regulations are an indication.[34] He seems deliberately to have rejected such a practice:

the disciples are to 'proclaim on the rooftops' what he has whispered in their ear (Matt. 10.27b; cf. Mark 4.22; Luke 8.17; also John 18.20). In the so-called 'cry of jubilation', Jesus thanks the Father because he has concealed his revelation from the wise (probably a reference to the scribes) and revealed it to 'babes'. The isolation of the saying Matt. 11.27; Luke 10.22 in the synoptic gospels seems to indicate that this kind of communication was made only occasionally to all the disciples. In the Gospel of John it is in the foreground, whereas in the synoptic gospels it emerges only sporadically. Might we not have a special kind of teaching here? It would not be secret, or systematically withheld from the majority of disciples, but it would have been more intimate teaching which not all the disciples knew (and which they may barely have understood).[35] The author of the Gospel of John may then have developed it *freely*, in the way that we know, but still keeping Jesus' teaching as a foundation. I only raise these as questions, but they are worth discussing.

In any case, they seem to me to show that there is no insuperable psychological difficulty in supposing that an eyewitness could speak of the unity of Jesus with God and of his pre-existence and allow himself to go on to speak in the place of Jesus. We must also keep in mind the unusual bond which some of Jesus' sayings about his special filial consciousness created between him and the disciples, incomparably beyond other relationships between rabbis and their pupils.

Another difficulty seems to arise when we ask whether an eyewitness who lived close to Jesus could extend the life of Jesus into the life of the community in characteristic Johannine fashion and see the incarnate and the exalted Jesus together in the Johannine *perspective*. Is an eyewitness capable of such detachment? We might remember here that the author only wrote the Gospel at the end of his life. But this explanation is not adequate. Rather, I shall repeat a remark I made earlier, which seems to me enough to remove the difficulty. As the group to which the author belongs was compelled *to defend the legitimacy of its special tradition about the events and its theology, rooted in heterodox Judaism*, it must almost of necessity have had to show that its community was *willed by Jesus*, and that there is a continuity between the incarnate Jesus and this group, that a line leads from one to the other. In the light of this *historical necessity* it is even more understandable that an *eyewitness, above all,* should adopt the particular perspective of the Johannine account of the life of Jesus.

As soon as we abandon the attempt to identify the eyewitness with John the son of Zebedee and include him in a group which comes from marginal Judaism, most of the difficulties fall away, or at least are considerably diminished. That the disciple belonged to the Twelve should be abandoned as a starting point, whether for affirming or denying that the Gospel was written by an eyewitness. For the Gospel's own testimony speaks clearly against this. The three great Johannine scholars of recent times, F. M. Braun, R. E. Brown and R. Schnackenburg, have evidently taken account of this fact, and for this reason none of them claims that the beloved disciple, whom they identify with John the son of Zebedee, wrote the Gospel. But as each wishes in some way to maintain the tradition going back to Irenaeus that the son of Zebedee wrote the Gospel, they have to assign to the eyewitness, who (they believe) has to be the apostle John, the more modest and in any case vague role of an authority standing behind the real evangelist.[36]

We have seen that the Irenaeus tradition can hardly be sustained in this very weakened form.[37] It cannot be assumed that the real author and his whole group could have chosen as the authority for their account of the life of Jesus a disciple who, from all that we know about him, differed so much from their own views.

However, we have one last question to put. Must we rule out *a priori* the *other* possibility, that the *anonymous* disciple, who is *not* identical with the son of Zebedee as we have characterized him, may only have been an authority to whom the real author and his circle referred? In other words, can we put forward the theory of an authority to explain the anonymous (beloved) disciple who was not one of the Twelve, even though we have rejected it in the case of John the son of Zebedee? As in this case the characteristics of the authority would coincide with those of the evangelist, we could at least in principle answer the question affirmatively, especially as we know that this kind of practice was not unknown, of writing a book under the patronage either of a prophetic figure in the Old Testament or of an apostolic figure in the New Testament.

Among the canonical gospels one might cite the Gospel of Mark as an example, if the quotation from Papias is right in stating that it is based on the testimony of the apostle Peter. However, in the case of Mark the composition of the Gospel would have been ascribed not to the authority, Peter, but to the man (Mark) who wrote the book. The Gospel of Matthew might be chosen as a better analogy, if the theory is correct that it was written by an author who drew on the testimony of the apostle Matthew, and therefore gave the latter's name to the work. In that case, in John, as in Matthew (and not as in the apocryphal gospels), there would be a real and not a fictitious connection between the author and the authority.

However, the case of the Gospel of John would also be different from that of Matthew in that here the authority would not be a known disciple but an *anonymous* one. In that case the anonymity of the beloved disciple would be more difficult, if not impossible, to explain. If an author refers to an authority, it is more natural for him to give a name than to keep silent. Furthermore, we should ask whether the redactor who in 21.24 said that the beloved disciple was identical with the author did not go too far – despite all that we know about pseudonymity in antiquity – in affirming immediately after some *very specific* remarks about the disciple, that this disciple 'wrote down' (γράψας) these things, when he knew that in fact they had been written down by someone else?

I would therefore prefer to leave the distinction between author and authority out of account, especially as in any case the role of this authority is quite undefined alongside the clear-cut literary and theological personality of the author.

I think that I have demonstrated that the beloved disciple was not the son of Zebedee and was not one of the Twelve. If he was the eye-witness of certain events and relies on traditions for others, and if his work has been revised by a circle of redactors belonging to his group, there is no need to make an already complex question even more complex by introducing an authority distinct from the author (although this possibility cannot be ruled out of account completely).

The assumption that the author is identical with the beloved disciple and is therefore a disciple of Jesus, though he comes from Judaea and belongs to a special group of disciples who derive from a different form of Judaism from that of the Twelve, has consequences for the possibility of tracing the 'Johannine circle' back into the time of Jesus. We may now raise a question which has emerged at several different points in the course of our investigation, namely how he is related to Jesus. We shall attempt to discuss it in a short summary, which will be the content of the next chapter.

IX

THE 'JOHANNINE CIRCLE' AND THE HISTORICAL JESUS

I T IS IMPOSSIBLE to write a really continuous history of the early Christian group which we have named the 'Johannine circle'. We have no direct sources for that. We have only been able to arrive at the results indicated so far by means of inferences. Nevertheless, these allow us to venture the attempt to trace *backwards* to their origin possible stages in a way from the already developed community which can be seen most clearly in the Gospel of John and in the Johannine Epistles.

In its developed form, we may term the 'Johannine circle' a church. We have seen[1] that different designations have been used: *ecclesiola*, church, sect. The last of these three is in any case somewhat misleading, as it goes against the concern of the group to maintain links with other Christians, for all the stress on and defence of its special character.

The group certainly had the structure of a community at the time when the Gospel of John and the Johannine Epistles were written. This is indicated by the role of baptism and the eucharist, which is certainly more developed here than in the rest of early Christianity. In this community, the *basic* liturgical *notion* that the presence of God, the 'glory', has been detached from the temple and cannot be localized in one place, led to a greater fixity of the new liturgical forms in which Christ was experienced as crucified and risen. These were baptism and the eucharist.[2] In contrast to the situation in the rest of Christianity, these forms did not first gain their complete significance with geographical remoteness from the Jerusalem temple and its destruction; from the beginning they grew so to speak organically from the whole theology of the Johannine circle.[3]

A number of things justify us in speaking of a Johannine 'community' or 'church'. An explicit interest in mission and polemic against false teaching, together with a constant concern to demonstrate the legitimacy of the group are some of them. If we now attempt to trace a way back from this more or less well-structured community to the beginnings, the first stage is the Jerusalem 'Hellenists', who were indeed members of the early community but already had their own organization and put forward their own liturgical theology which rejected any fixing of the divine presence in one place. To begin with, we can only conjecture a further connection between them and a special group of disciples distinct from the Twelve, which already existed in the lifetime of Jesus. This, however, is suggested by the fact that these Hellenists seem to have belonged to the earliest community in Jerusalem from the beginning. The affinity of the Johannine circle to heterodox marginal Judaism is another feature which allows us to trace its origin further back into this heterodox Judaism. One historical link (which is probably not the only one) is evident between this Judaism and the hypothetical group of disciples: the movement of John the Baptist, to which the Johannine circle is closely related, as the Gospel shows.

We thus arrive at the following line, moving back in time: Johannine community – special Hellenist group in the early community in Jerusalem – Johannine circle of disciples – disciples of the Baptist – heterodox marginal Judaism. However, one link is missing between the Johannine circle of disciples and the Baptist's disciples; not any link, but a fundamental one: Jesus. At an earlier stage in this work I have pointed out[4] that there is often a tendency in Johannine scholarship today to evaluate the Johannine circle only as an element of syncretism without taking into account the historical Jesus at all.

Of course this judgment is partly conditioned by a dogmatic exclusion of the Gospel of John as a source for the knowledge of the historical Jesus. We have seen that the Johannine integrated view of the life of Jesus and the community influenced the account of events and the preaching of Jesus in the Gospel of John far more strongly than the form-critical, traditio-critical or redaction-critical trend of the synoptic gospels, and that therefore it is difficult to use the Gospel of John as a historical source. At the same time, however, we have established that it is illegitimate to exclude it completely, since in a number of passages unprejudiced exegesis compels us to prefer the Johannine account to that of the synoptics.

As, however, the Gospel of John is our chief source for a knowledge of the Johannine circle, and as in this chapter we wish to discover the relationship of this circle to the historical Jesus, this means that at the same time we are concerned with the relationship of the Gospel of John to the historical Jesus.[5] To avoid begging the question, we shall take the synoptic gospels as the chief source of knowledge of the 'historical Jesus', though without excluding the information in the Gospel of John in the case of obvious exceptions.

It seems to me to be necessary to put the question seriously and not to take a negative answer for granted from the beginning. The long chapter about the author of the Gospel of John suggests it to us. Our remarks have implicitly indicated a continuous link between the Johannine circle and Jesus through the beloved disciple. The result remains the same, even if this disciple were really only an 'authority'. But it should also be remembered that the aim of the whole Gospel is to draw a line from the life of the incarnate Jesus to the church and to the Johannine community in particular.

Might all this be mere fiction? Having raised this question from the perspective of the problem of authorship, we shall now look at it once again from the standpoint of our attempt to sketch the origin and development of the Johannine circle. In what follows I shall attempt to illuminate the problem from two sides in succession, by summing up hints that have already been given, considering first Jesus and heterodox Judaism and then Jesus and the Johannine circle (and its earlier stages).

Obviously we cannot demonstrate a definite historical connection here between marginal Judaism and Jesus, as the synoptics themselves go back to traditions with disciples as authorities, which were not in direct contact with that Judaism. We shall therefore primarily look for an inner relationship between Jesus and this Judaism and the characteristic aspects of the Johannine circle. If these are to be found, it will also be legitimate at least to consider the possibility of more direct links.

1. *Jesus and heterodox Judaism*

It has always been assumed that certain apocalyptic views were cherished in a more or less esoteric Judaism, even if that Judaism was not directly heterodox. This is the setting above all for the rather mysterious late-Jewish speculations about the Son of Man, which still present problems despite the numerous references to them. We are constantly reminded of them by the particularly frequent use of the phrase 'Son of Man' not only in the synoptic gospels but also in John. Following Bultmann, scholars have questioned whether Jesus used the title Son of Man at all as a designation of himself – he is said to have spoken of a coming Son of Man who would be different from himself – but this has not been proved,[6] and in any case, no matter how Jesus spoke of the Son of Man, he took up conceptions which were not commonly current in Judaism. Some writers have even suggested secret teaching.[7]

When we speak of marginal Jewish communities or sects, we tend today to think first of all of Qumran. Immediately after the discovery of the Qumran scrolls, exaggerated claims were made and presented as a journalistic sensation: it was said that the whole of Christianity had been anticipated in the Qumran sect and that Christianity did not introduce anything fundamentally new. Since then, however, a reaction has rightly set in on the part of scholars who have recognized the influence of Qumran on the rise of Christianity but have contrasted the proclamation of Jesus with the teaching and instructions of the sect. In fact Jesus' freedom towards the law is in direct contradiction to the exaggerated legalism of the Qumran people. However, in distinguishing Jesus from Qumran, scholars have probably over-corrected and gone too far in the opposite direction. Qumran sheds light not only on certain aspects of the teaching of Jesus in John but also on his synoptic teaching. The attitude of Jesus to the temple, which we shall discuss later, also finds points of contact in Qumran, although the orientation is different.[8] If Jesus followed the Qumran calendar,[9] there would be an external feature in common here. The ritual washings in Qumran should certainly be distinguished from the single baptism of John the Baptist. But the activity of John the

Baptist also belongs in the framework of the late-Jewish baptismal movement.

We have more than hypotheses in connection with the relationship between Jesus and *the disciples of John the Baptist*. The whole of the early Christian tradition, both Johannine and synoptic, agrees that Jesus' appearance is directly connected with that of John the Baptist. We could infer indirectly from the synoptic gospels what is said explicitly in the Gospel of John (1.35ff.): Jesus began his activity in the milieu of the Baptist and among his disciples, and was probably one of them himself.[10] Here, at any rate, is one of the connecting links between Jesus and marginal Judaism, and especially the Johannine circle.

We have seen that there are clear connections between the Johannine circle and *Samaria*. Can we also trace these back to Jesus? In the light of Matt. 10.5 we might be tempted to give a negative answer: 'Do not go into cities of the Samaritans.' As it is difficult to reconcile the saying with the universalism of Jesus, its authenticity has been doubted or disputed.[11] But even if it is, as I think, genuine, the Fourth Evangelist is evidently concerned to rule out any false conclusions which could be drawn from an instruction of this kind. In telling of the meeting between Jesus and the woman of Samaria (ch. 4) he stresses Jesus' will that the seed sown there by Jacob's well in Sychar should issue in the later mission to this area and bring forth fruit.[12] In addition, in a series of stories in Luke, Jesus also shows an emphatic interest in the Samaritans: in the parable of the good Samaritan (Luke 10.25ff.), in his abrupt rejection of the request of the sons of Zebedee that vengeance should be taken on the Samaritan city because of its hostile attitude to them (Luke 9.51ff.), and also in the singling out of the Samaritan among the ten lepers (Luke 17.11ff.).[13]

Luke and the author of the Fourth Gospel had special traditions about the relationship of Jesus to the Samaritans. The taunt 'You are a Samaritan', addressed to Jesus in John 8.48 and coupled with the charge that he had a demon, presupposes a general awareness that Jesus had special sympathy for the Samaritans. His return to Ephraim, a city under Samaritan influence, could also be connected with this (John 11.54).

Jesus' critical attitude to the temple also comes into consideration here. This puts him quite near to most of the representatives of heterodox Judaism. Certainly he is far removed from the policy of playing off Gerizim against the temple in Jerusalem, and far removed also from the polemic of the Qumran sect in favour of a new temple, different from the existing one but again to be made by human hands.[14] He purifies the temple, but does not attempt to abolish it by human force. The saying in the Sermon on the Mount, 'When you bring your gift' (Matt. 5.23), still presupposes the temple cult. And yet Jesus had contact with marginal Judaism in so far as he did not regard the temple as an ultimate institution and prophesied its end (Mark 13.1).

Jesus must have said something about the destruction of the temple, since otherwise his words could hardly have been distorted by witnesses at his trial to the effect that he had said that he himself would destroy the temple. The *second* half of the (false) witness borne against Jesus probably corresponds to an actual saying of his, that he would 'build a temple not made with human hands' (Mark 14.58); other sayings of his suggest that this was a reference to the eschatological community of disciples. John 2.19 probably contains the *first* part of the authentic logion underlying the testimony, in a more correct form: 'Destroy (not, '*I* will destroy,' as the false witnesses of Mark 14.57f. put it) this temple and I will build another.' This simply means, 'If this temple is destroyed, I will build a new one.'[15]

If Jesus himself is not a stranger to marginal Judaism, without having belonged to it directly, we can understand better why he cannot be claimed too exclusively for synoptic and Pauline Christianity; there is much to connect him with Johannine Christianity also, which is rooted in that particular kind of Judaism.

2. *Jesus and the Johannine circle (or its predecessors)*

The last-mentioned example of Jesus' attitude to the temple allows us to recognize a link not only between Jesus and heterodox Judaism, but also between Jesus and the Johannine circle. In the story of the cleansing of the temple, the Fourth Evangelist deliberately and emphatically goes beyond what he claims Jesus to have said in that situation. He remarks explicitly that the disciples (among whom he probably includes himself) only 'recalled' (to use the Johannine interpretation) the saying of Jesus after Jesus' death. He can therefore develop Jesus' saying on the lines of the basic Johannine conception that 'the presence of God is now realized in the person of Jesus', by applying it to the body of Christ. He is convinced that in so doing he is reproducing the view of Jesus himself: 'But he was speaking of the temple of his body.' Is this conviction justified? Jesus certainly did not make the identification 'temple' = 'his own body', but at all events the view of the Johannine circle that the temple had been done away with by the person of the Logos – Son of Man is not very far from Jesus' expectation that the temple will one day be replaced as a place of worship by the eschatological community of the disciples.

The frequency of the term Son of Man in the Fourth Gospel has often been stressed.[16] In this connection, too, a line can be drawn to all that we can infer from the synoptic gospels about Jesus' predilection for this title, which (as we have seen) probably had its origin in a special Jewish doctrine. The way in which Jesus speaks of himself and his unity with God in the Gospel of John is certainly part of that rethinking and reinterpretation which the evangelist believes to be legitimate. But the evangelist is not concerned to dispute all the sayings in the synoptic gospels where Jesus is speaking of his special relationship with the Father, in connection with his own awareness of himself. Nevertheless, the sayings of Jesus were developed and interpreted by the Johannine circle and the author; we might even suppose that at least in one point there was a connection between the prologue to the Gospel and Jesus himself. If according to the synoptic gospels, too, Jesus really regarded himself as the primal 'wisdom', which had been rejected,[17] a figure which plays such a considerable role in certain circles of late Judaism, it would be particularly understandable why the prologue to the Fourth Gospel, as is generally assumed, has transferred ideas about 'wisdom' and perhaps even a wisdom hymn to the Logos made flesh in Christ.

But we must now raise the further question whether there are signs that in addition to those disciples who came from official Judaism, Jesus also had others from marginal Judaism to whom he had a rather different (though not fundamentally different) relationship which might also be expressed in a different form of instruction.

It seems to me difficult to dispute the synoptic account according to which Jesus chose the Twelve out of the crowd of disciples, although the attempt has been made and has something to be said for it.[18] However, this choice certainly did not mean that discipleship was limited to the Twelve. The probable explanation for the exclusive position which the Twelve occupy in the synoptic gospels is that the synoptic tradition mainly derives from them. Luke mentions the sending out of seventy (seventy-two) disciples only briefly (Luke 10.1), but in so doing does, of course, break with this tradition. We have seen that in John the Twelve hardly appear as a group at all, and that other intimate disciples of Jesus make an appearance. Even according to the synoptic gospels, then, did Jesus have two kinds of disciples, one of which came from official Judaism and the other from a more or less heterodox Judaism?

The geographical homeland of the Twelve was Galilee. However, even in the synoptic gospels, especially in Luke, we find indications that Jesus had friends in Jerusalem.

The synoptic gospels also suggest that the former disciples of John the Baptist, whom Jesus may have known when he was close to the Baptist, included some who came from Judaea and above all some who came from more or less non-conformist Judaism. These attached themselves to Jesus without accompanying him all the time. Perhaps this hypothesis can be reconciled with Luke's somewhat obscure note about the sending out of the seventy (seventy-two) disciples. As, according to Luke, Jesus is probably thinking of the seventy nations mentioned in Gen. 10, these are connected with the mission extending beyond Israel. Be this as it may, it is probably reasonable to assume that the wider circle of disciples also contained those who later formed the group of 'Hellenists' in the early church in Jerusalem, especially when we consider the early date at which they belonged to the primitive church.[19] The rapid spread of belief in Christ can be better explained if it had already been propagated by a number of groups of disciples even during Jesus' lifetime.

If Jesus himself was not far removed from heterodox Judaism, we may assume that he also found disciples who were closely connected with that Judaism. Another consideration suggests that it is not improbable that the relationship between Jesus and his disciples could take different forms depending on circumstances. The synoptics disclose that even among the Twelve Jesus made a certain choice depending on the situation. If, as we have reason to suppose, the wider circle of disciples included two groups of rather different Jewish origin, Jesus will certainly have directed his preaching in a similar fashion. Far be it from me to claim that the Johannine discourses as we have them are the one form of this preaching. We have seen how the later Johannine circle and the author of the Gospel felt justified and indeed called to develop Jesus' preaching in respect of their aim by a process of interpretative 'recollection'. However, Jesus may still have spoken in different ways with different people on some subjects. He will certainly also have had disciples from *both* groups around him. We should not envisage them as having been completely separate. I have pointed out continually that the synoptic gospels themselves have a saying from Q with a 'Johannine' ring (Matt. 11.27; Luke 10.22), which stands out like an erratic block. Is there not a recollection even in the synoptics that Jesus spoke about some things only rarely, and in a special way?

We have seen[20] that he rejected secret doctrines of the kind to be found in the Jewish sects. Nevertheless, it is probable that he himself did not speak to all the disciples in the same way. In particular, all the sayings relating to his understanding of himself probably belong with a much more intimate form of preaching; they are veiled in the synoptic gospels with a remarkable restraint.[21] In this connection we have also mentioned the hypothesis of two forms of instruction put forward by H. Riesenfeld and B. Gerhardsson, albeit in another context.[22] In Jerusalem, and with his approaching death, Jesus may well have revealed certain things about which he did not speak elsewhere.

At all events, we should not be too hasty to dismiss the claim of the Johannine circle and the appeal to Jesus himself which is presupposed in the Gospel of John as being irreconcilable with our knowledge about the 'historical Jesus'. Were it accepted, two groups of disciples would go back to Jesus. One would be more important by virtue of its number and the continuity of its common life, and would be represented by Peter; the other, represented by the beloved disciple, would be smaller and rest on a more inward relationship. Were this to be so, our customary picture of the beginnings of Christianity would have to be revised in this direction.

X

APPENDIX:
HYPOTHESES ABOUT THE DATE AND
PLACE OF ORIGIN OF THE GOSPEL OF JOHN

WE MUST DISTINGUISH the composition of the Gospel and its redaction from the origin of the Johannine circle.

1. *Date*

We may conclude indirectly from the Gospel itself (John 21.24) that the Gospel was edited some time after it was 'written'. As the person (or persons) speaking there in the first person plural gave the Gospel its present form, the question of date is as complicated as that of authorship. However, whereas the contents of the Gospel give us some help towards solving the question of authorship, the hypothetical character of all the indications of date is much greater. Only with such a proviso can we venture an attempt in this direction.

First of all we must determine the chronological distance between the anonymous disciple and the redactor whose voice can be heard in ch. 21. We can only say with certainty that the disciple was dead at the time when the redactor(s) did their work. They had to counter the view that 'the disciple would not die'. However, we cannot determine how much time elapsed after his death. One is tempted to assume that the event was not too far back in the past, as the problem still seems to be a vivid one, raised by the departure of the last of the eyewitnesses. Tradition is probably wrong in identifying the author with John the son of Zebedee, but it does speak of the considerable *age* which the disciple reached,[1] and this would explain the origin of the rumour that the disciple would not die.

(a) Date of redaction

Even if we do not put the date of the editing and revision by the redactor too far from the death of the author, we must still put it towards the end of the first century. Scholars who rule out any relationship between the redactor and an eyewitness (e.g. A. Loisy, A. Schweitzer) go even further, some as late as 120–140.[2] However, the late attestation of the Gospel used to support this assumption does not justify such a late dating. Of course we have no certain relevant text before the second half of the second century. Nevertheless, there is much to suggest that Ignatius of Antioch used the Gospel at the beginning of the second century without citing it, as C. Maurer believes.[3] The same is true for Justin Martyr, though he is only writing about 150. On the other hand, it is uncertain whether the author of I Clement (c. 96) knew the Gospel, as M.-E. Boismard assumes.[4] The reason why it was seldom cited, and at a late date, will be that for a long time the Johannine circle was more or less separate from mainstream Christianity.

The Gospel soon circulated widely in gnostic circles. However, this does not allow us to put the origin of its redaction about the time of the great gnostic schools of the second century. As the Johannine circle has its origin in a heterodox Judaism, it is not surprising that this type of Christianity fell in most closely with the tendencies of gnosticism, which has common roots with it.[5] Hence, too, the mistrust which the Gospel often encountered. If we begin from the use of the Gospel, we shall also find ourselves putting the origin of its final form towards the end of the first century.

Now this approximate date can be specified in a more certain and objective way by means of the earliest papyri discovered in recent decades. These contain fragments of the text of John. The Ryland papyrus P 52, which comes from Egypt, contains John 18.31–33, 37f., and is unanimously put at the beginning of the second century (c. 130). Egerton Papyrus 2, which according to the most probable theory combines the synoptic gospels and John, belongs to approximately the same time.[6] If the Gospel was already known in Egypt at the beginning of the second century, it must have been edited some time before the two papyri were produced, i.e. earlier than the year 100.

(b) The date of the composition of the original Gospel

It is more difficult to give a firm date for the work of the evangelist himself. If the author is identical with the anonymous disciple who died in old age, he seems (as has already been suggested) to have written the Gospel in the last years of his life: or, to put it in a better way, he seems to have written it 'down' towards the end of his life. After all, it is also difficult to talk of the date of the Gospel because the author was probably engaged on his extensive work over a long period, and may have begun it relatively early.[7]

The dates of the synoptic gospels are hypothetical, but they are usually taken as a starting-point for determining that of the Gospel of John. As the priority of the synoptic gospels is usually assumed as a matter of course, and it is often supposed that the author of John at least knew Luke, the date of the Gospel of John is generally thought to be about 80 at the earliest. However, it seems to me more and more likely that the evangelist should be thought to be independent of the written synoptic gospels, if not the synoptic tradition. This starting point is therefore problematical. If we are right in seeing the author as eyewitness of at least some events, I am now inclined to change my earlier opinion and put the original composition of the Gospel at least as early as the synoptic gospels, and probably even earlier than the earliest of them.[8] None of them is written by an eyewitness.

This conclusion seems to offend against our customary views of the New Testament.[9] But in the context of the present work we have to begin from the fact that this group is a different group from mainstream Christianity, and *parallel* to it. This *parallelism* must also be considered in terms of *chronology*, whereas usually it is taken for granted that the relationship between the synoptic gospels and the Gospel of John is a chronological succession. If we put the hypothetical Q in the fifties, we cannot rule out *a priori* the assumption that the composition of the early stages of the Gospel of John is to be put before AD 70. However, we should not go back too far,[10] since according to the solution which I have suggested, the evangelist used traditions which in places indicate an advanced stage of development in connection with events to which he was not an eye-witness. We would therefore prefer not to attempt to give a more precise date.

2.   *Place of origin*

Uncertainty about the place of composition is even greater. We have seen that the home of the disciple was probably in Judaea. On the other hand, the Gospel is interested in Samaria. Is the place in which the redactor did his work the same as that in which the author spent the last part of his life? This is probable, if he edited the Gospel not long after the death of the evangelist. We are almost certainly to assume that both the group and the author moved at one time. Of the various hypotheses which have been put forward there are two which possess a greater degree of probability. First of all, *Syria*. We know that a Judaism with syncretistic tendencies developed here. The Odes of Solomon come from this area. Furthermore, of all the writings of the apostolic fathers, the letters of Ignatius show the greatest affinity to the Gospel of John. Whether we follow C. Maurer[11] in assuming that Ignatius knew the Gospel, or H. Köster[12] in supposing that because of the theological differences they can only have worked in a similar milieu, Syria can be seen as a region common to both authors. Assuming (as we have) that Ignatius was part of an already developed, later continuation of the Johannine circle, the differences indicated can be reconciled with a knowledge of the Gospel. The more or less bilingual country of Syria would also fit well with what we have said about the Semitic character of the Greek of the Gospel.

The other possibility which can be supported with strong (perhaps even stronger) arguments is *Transjordania*. This was the land of syncretism, and above all of the baptist movements. According to traditions which have been disputed but not disproved, many Christians fled here after AD 70, probably with the remnants of the Qumran sect who, according to my reckoning,[13] were taken up into a heretical Jewish Christianity which was all too open to a certain type of Jewish gnosticism. This is attested by the Pseudo-Clementines. If the sect of John the Baptist in particular had settled in this area, we could see why it was attacked by both the Jewish Christians of the Pseudo-Clementines and the Fourth Gospel, albeit in quite different ways.[14]

I need mention only briefly the two other regions which have been conjectured as possible places of origin. The arguments used in support of them seem much less well founded than those for Syria and Transjordania. First of all, *Egypt*. Alexandria has been suggested, especially when parallels were drawn almost exclusively between the ideas of Philo and the prologue, to define the milieu of the Gospel more closely. However, we now know that the cultural setting is much wider than that. Additional support has been looked for from the fact that the first copies of the text of John are papyri which were discovered in Egypt. However, as conditions in Egypt favour the preservation of papyri, this argument is not a particularly valuable one.

Since antiquity, *Asia Minor* has been seen as the home of the Gospel of John. This tradition is linked with that which sees John the son of Zebedee as the author. However, it could also be considered independently. In its favour, the presence in Asia Minor of the heresies attacked in the Gospel of John, and in particular of a group of disciples of John, has been noted. It is also pointed out that the seer in the Revelation of John was on Patmos (though this argument presupposes a solution to the problem of the relationship between this book and the Gospel).[15] The fact that each of these theories can be supported by reasonable arguments and the resultant uncertainty is expressed in the various attempts to link them together by saying that the author moved his place of abode several times.[16]

BIBLIOGRAPHY

More has been written in recent decades about the Gospel of John than about any other book of the Bible. Only the works which are particularly important for the present study have been quoted in the notes. Many more are, of course, relevant. We are fortunate to have not only the account of scholarship by E. Haenchen in *TR* 23, 1955, pp. 295ff., but also three other very valuable bibliographies;

E. Malatesta, *St John's Gospel 1920–1965. A cumulative and classified bibliography of books and periodical literature on the Fourth Gospel* (Analecta Biblica 1967).

A. Moda, 'Quarto Vangelo 1966–72', *Rivista Biblica Italiana* 22, 1974, pp. 53ff.

H. Thyen, 'Aus der Literatur zum Johannesevangelium (mit einer Bibliographie seit 1966 und einer ausgewählten von 1956–1966)', *TR* 40, 1974, pp. 1ff.

The following is a selected list of the *more recent commentaries* which are cited in the notes simply as 'commentary':

B. F. Westcott, *The Gospel according to St John* (two vols), 1887 (new edition by A. Fox 1958)

A. Loisy, *Le quatrième évangile et les épîtres dites de Jean*, 1903, ²1921

T. Zahn, *Das Evangelium des Johannes*, ⁶1921

W. Bauer, *Das Johannesevangelium erklärt*, HNT, 1925, ²1933

M. J. Lagrange, *L'évangile selon S. Jean*, EB, 1925, ²1936

J. H. Bernard, *A Critical and Exegetical Commentary according to St John* (2 vols), ICC, 1928

G. H. C. Macgregor, *The Gospel of John*, Moffatt, 1929

A. Schlatter, *Der Evangelist Johannes. Wie er spricht, denkt und glaubt*, 1930 (reprinted)

E. Hoskyns, *The Fourth Gospel*, ed. F. N. Davey, 1940, ²1947

R. Bultmann, *The Gospel of John* (1941), 1971

A. Wikenhauser, *Das Evangelium nach Johannes*, RNT, 1949, ³1961

H. Strathmann, *Das Evangelium nach Johannes*, NTD, 1951

C. K. Barrett, *The Gospel according to St John*, 1954 (reprinted)

R. H. Lightfoot, *St John's Gospel*, ed. C. F. Evans, 1956

A. Richardson, *The Gospel according to St John*, TBC, 1959

A. van den Bussche, *Het vierde evangelie* (4 vols.), 1959/60

J. N. Sanders, *A Commentary on the Gospel according to St John*, completed by
    B. A. Mastin, 1968

R. E. Brown, *The Gospel according to St John*, Anchor Bible, I, 1966; II,
    1970

R. Schnackenburg, *The Gospel according to St John*, Herder's Theological
    Commentary, I, 1968

L. Morris, *The Gospel according to John*, 1972

B. Lindars, *The Gospel of John*, NCB, 1972

S. Schultz, *Das Evangelium nach Johannes*, NTD, 1972

NOTES

Chapter One

1. J. Wellhausen, *Das Evangelium Johannis*, 1908 (assumes a basic document, *Grundschrift*. So too does F. Spitta, *Das Johannesevangelium als Quelle des Lebens Jesu*, 1910, see below, p. 120 n. 10, but his historical evaluation is quite different).

2. E. Schwartz, *Aporien im 4.Evangelium*, 1907/8.

3. So also, among others, F. M. Braun, *Jean le Théologien et son évangile dans l'Eglise ancienne*, 1959, pp. 24f. However, the fact that ch. 21 was only appended and not inserted into ch. 20 seems to indicate that chs. 1–20 were taken to be essentially finished and that the plan of the Gospel was felt to be established. So too B. Lindars, *Behind the Fourth Gospel*, 1971, p. 18.

4. J. Becker, 'Die Abschiedsreden Jesu im Johannesevangelium', *ZNW* 61, 1970, p. 215, distinguishes several redactions here.

5. W. Wilkens, *Die Entstehungsgeschichte des 4. Evangeliums*, 1958.

6. See his commentary, p. xxxvi (the fourth of the stages of development which he posits).

7. Commentary, p. xxiv.

8. See his commentary, pp. 11ff.

9. See A. Moda, 'Quarto Vangelo 1966–1972', *Rivista Biblica Italiana* 22, 1974, pp. 53ff., and H. Thyen's bibliography in 'Aus der Literatur zum Johannesevangelium', *TR* 40, 1974, pp. 4ff.

10. So also E. Meyer, *Ursprung und Anfänge des Christentums* I, 1921, pp. 310f.

11. E. Schweizer, *Ego Eimi*, 1939. In a 'Survey of several decades of scholarly work' in the Preface to the Second Edition, 1965, the author maintains his theory but makes an exception for the prologue and the miracle stories.

12. E. Ruckstuhl, *Die literarische Einheit des Johannesevangeliums*, 1951.

13. C. K. Barrett in his commentary exercises great restraint, as to some degree does Wellhausen, op. cit. (towards delimiting a *Grundschrift*).

14. See P. Gardner-Smith, *St John and the Synoptic Gospels*, 1938. C. K. Barrett in his commentary and W. G. Kümmel, *Introduction to the New*

Testament, [2]1975, pp. 202f., assume that it is dependent on Mark and Luke; R. M. Grant, 'The Fourth Gospel and the Church', *HTR* 35, 1942, pp. 95ff. that it is dependent only on Mark.

15. The Lukan parallels in particular show common features, especially in the passion narrative. J. A. Bailey, *The Traditions common to the Gospels of Luke and John*, 1963, assumes that the Gospel of John is dependent on Luke. M.-E. Boismard, 'St Luc et la rédaction du 4e évangile', *RB* 69, 1962, pp. 185ff., identifies the final redactor with Luke himself.

16. Above all A. Faure, 'Die alttestamentliche Zitate im 4. Evangelium und die Quellenscheidungshypothese', *ZNW* 21, 1922, pp. 99ff.

17. R. T. Fortna, *The Gospel of Signs. A Reconstruction of the Narrative Source underlying the Fourth Gospel*, 1970. J. Becker, 'Wunder und Christologie', *NTS* 1969/70, pp. 130ff., also presupposes the *semeia* source, and is concerned to bring out its theological purpose. See also A. Dauer, *Die Passionsgeschichte im Johannesevangelium*, 1972, who reconstructs a source for the passion narrative in a similar way.

18. H. Becker, *Die Reden des Johannesevangeliums und der Stil der gnostischen Offenbarungsrede*, 1956. See also the account of scholarship by J. M. Robinson, 'The Johannine Trajectory', in H. Koester and J. M. Robinson, *Trajectories through Early Christianity*, 1971, pp. 232ff.

19. But see the qualification which E. Schweizer makes to his own theory in connection with the miracle stories, n. 11 above.

20. C. H. Dodd, *The Interpretation of the Fourth Gospel*, 1953.

21. B. Noack, *Zur johanneischen Tradition*, 1954.

22. For this attempt see O. Merlier, *Le 4e évangile. La question johannique*, 1961.

23. Is it not in a sense the *lectio difficilior* and as such original?

24. R. E. Brown, commentary, p. xxxiv.

25. *A posteriori* it may, of course, be necessary for exegetes to make corrections to this scheme in the course of their explanation and in places to make it more precise.

26. That is not to say that they are therefore unnecessary.

Chapter Two

1. E. Käsemann, *The Testament of Jesus*, 1968. He defines Johannine theology as 'naive docetism'. See the detailed criticism by G. Bornkamm, 'Zur Interpretation des Johannesevangeliums. Eine Auseinandersetzung mit E. Käsemanns Schrift *Jesu letzter Wille nach Joh. 17*', *Geschichte und Glaube, Gesammelte Aufsätze* III, pp. 104ff. See p. 108, n. 29 below.

2. L. Schottroff, 'Heil als innerweltliche Entweltlichung. Der gnostische Hintergrund der johanneische Vorstellung vom Zeitpunkt der Erlösung', *NT* 11, 1969, pp. 294ff.; id., *Der Glaubende und die feindliche Welt. Beobachtungen zum gnostischen Dualismus und seiner Bedeutung für Paulus und Johannes*, 1970, and on this E. Ruckstuhl, 'Das Johannesevangelium und die

Gnosis', in *Neues Testament und Geschichte, Festschrift für O. Cullmann*, 1972, pp. 143ff.

3. See below, p. 33 and especially pp. 35ff.

4. See below, pp. 18ff.

5. H. Windisch, *Johannes und die Synoptiker*, 1926.

6. J. L. Martyn, *History and Theology in the Fourth Gospel*, 1968.

7. J. A. T. Robinson, 'The Destination and Purpose of St John's Gospel', *NTS* 6, 1959/60, pp. 117ff.: W. C. van Unnik, 'The Purpose of St John's Gospel', *Studia Evangelica*, 1959, pp. 382ff.

8. B. Rigaux, 'Les destinataires du 4e évangile à la lumière de Jean 17', *Revue Théologique de Louvain* 1, 1970, pp. 289ff., thinks especially of initiates.

9. See O. Cullmann, *Salvation in History*, 1967, pp. 278ff. For salvation-historical thought in John see also W. G. Kümmel, 'Heilsgeschichte im Neuen Testament?', in *Neues Testament und Kirche. Festschrift für R. Schnackenburg*, 1974, pp. 455f.

10. E. Käsemann, 'Zum johanneischen Verfasserproblem', *ZTK* 48, 1951, p. 302.

11. The redactor may have called the anonymous disciple 'the beloved disciple' for this reason. See p. 74 below.

12. See pp. 48f. below.

13. See p. 61 below.

14. O. Cullmann, *Early Christian Worship*, SBT 10, 1953.

15. For a recent study on the sacraments see H. Klos, *Die Sakramente im Johannesevangelium*, 1970. See the following note.

16. The objections which have been made against my work and repeated in stereotyped fashion in the commentaries and other publications partly arise from the fact that this work is deliberately concerned only with this one expression of community life. I did not mean to say that it was the only aspect of the presence of Christ in the community. Even H. Klos, op. cit., includes me among those for whom the sacraments play the dominant role in the Fourth Gospel. Otherwise he takes a middle course in his generally good survey of the directions of exegesis; the gospel is neither 'anti-sacramental' (Bultmann) nor 'emphatically sacramental' (p. 94).

17. O. Cullmann, 'Der johanneische Gebrauch doppeldeutiger Ausdrücke als Schlüssel zum Verständnis des 4. Evangeliums', *TZ* 4, 1948, 360ff.

18. The argument is valid even if the remark is a gloss, as there is still a reference to the cross.

19. The farewell discourses, or at any rate chs. 15–17, are often assigned to a redactor chiefly for literary reasons (see p. 3 above): thus already J. Wellhausen, op. cit., pp. 62ff.: E. Meyer, op. cit., pp. 310f.: also by G. Richter, 'Die Deutung des Kreuzestodes in der Leidensgeschichte des Johannesevangeliums', *Bibel und Leben* 9, 1968, pp. 21ff., and lastly by J. Becker, 'Abschiedsreden' (p. 102, n. 4 above), who thinks of 'a pupil of

the evangelist' who 'in shifting the accent remains relatively close to the discourse of his teacher'. Others, e.g. C. H. Dodd, *The Interpretation of the Fourth Gospel*, pp. 390ff., and C. K. Barrett, commentary, pp. 397ff., assume that the insertion was made by a disciple, but that the text of the insertion comes from the evangelist.

20. W. Thüsing, *Die Erhöhung und Verherrlichung Jesu im Johannesevangelium*, 1959, [2]1970, also claims that the evangelist sees 'the significance of his writing' here (p. 159). For 'remembering' see O. Cullmann, *Early Christian Worship*, p. 49, and N. A. Dahl, 'Anamnesis', *Studia Theologica*, 1947, pp. 94ff.

21. In his article, 'Die Parakletenvorstellung im Johannesevangelium', *ZTK* 71, 1974, pp. 31ff., U. B. Müller also connects the Paraclete with the need for the Gospel to be legitimated, but this is in the context of his hypothesis of a development of the idea of the Paraclete corresponding to the literary division of the farewell discourses.

Chapter Three

1. I would stress this point. L. Morris, *Studies in the Fourth Gospel*, 1969, pp. 122ff., in the context of my explanation of the story of the woman of Samaria, wrongly ascribes to me the thought that this episode in the life of Jesus is *only* concerned with the life of the church.

2. See O. Cullmann, 'L'évangile johannique et l'histoire de salut', *NTS* 11, 1964/65, pp. 111ff., and the article by W. G. Kümmel cited above, p. 104, n. 9, pp. 455f.

3. O. Cullmann, 'Εἶδεν καὶ ἐπίστευσεν', *Festschrift für M. Goguel*, 1950, pp. 52ff. Also F. Hahn, 'Sehen und Glauben im Johannesevangelium', *Festschrift für O. Cullmann*, 1972, pp. 125ff., who has a broader understanding of 'seeing'. In terms of the concept of *martyria*, I. de la Potterie, *La notion de témoignage dans S. Jean*, 1959.

4. For the 'hour' see W. Thüsing, op. cit., p. 89 ('primarily the point in salvation history appointed by the Father').

5. How would the ancient historian manage if he showed the same scepticism as theologians and wanted to use all documents which deal with events, but show a particular bias, for information only about this bias, and not about the events? If we should also allow that a conviction of faith is prior to any other bias, there may be some justification in the question.

6. M. Goguel, *The Life of Jesus*, 1933: C. H. Dodd, *Historical Tradition in the Fourth Gospel*, 1963. See also A. J. B. Higgins, *The Historicity of the Fourth Gospel*, 1960. E. Renan builds his *Life of Jesus* on the narrative of the Fourth Gospel (and not on the discourses).

7. See R. D. Potter, 'Topography and Archeology in the Fourth Gospel', *Studia Evangelica*, 1959, pp. 328ff., and O. Merlier, *Itinéraires de Jésus et chronologie dans le 4ᵉ évangile*, 1961.

8. See O. Cullmann, *The State in the New Testament*, [2]1963, pp. 38ff.

9. According to H. Riesenfeld, 'The Gospel Tradition and its Beginnings', *Studia Evangelica*, 1959, and B. Gerhardsson, *Memory and Manuscript. Oral Tradition and Written Transmission in Rabbinic Judaism and Early Christianity*, [2]1964, we must distinguish between teaching of Jesus handed down according to rabbinic rules and other teaching which will have been freer. If this theory is correct, it could shed light on the formal side of this distinction. See pp. 93f. below.

Chapter Four

1. A. Schlatter, *Die Sprache und Heimat des vierten Evangelisten*, 1902.

2. K. Beyer, *Semitische Syntax im Neuen Testament* I, 1962, pp. 17f.

3. C. F. Burney, *The Aramaic Origin of the Fourth Gospel*, 1922.

4. M.-E. Boismard believes that some textual variants can be explained as translation errors.

5. C. C. Torrey, 'The Aramaic Origin of the Gospel of John', *HTR* 16, 1923, pp. 305ff.

6. J. de Zwaan, 'John wrote in Aramaic', *JBL* 57, 1938, pp. 155f.

7. Matthew Black, *An Aramaic Approach to the Gospels and Acts*, [3]1967.

8. E. C. Colwell, *The Greek of the Fourth Gospel* I, 1931, pp. 91ff.

9. See his commentary, pp. 128ff.

10. E. A. Abbott, *Johannine Vocabulary*, 1905.

11. P. Gaechter, 'Der formale Aufbau der Abschiedsreden Jesu', *ZTK* 42, 1934, pp. 155ff.: id., 'Die Form der eucharistischen Reden Jesu', *ZTK* 43, 1935, pp. 420ff.: id., 'Strophen im Johannesevangelium', *ZTK* 44, 1936, pp. 99ff., 402ff.

12. D. Mollat, 'L'Evangile de S. Jean', *Bible de Jérusalem*, [2]1960.

13. E. Haenchen, 'Probleme des johanneischen Prologs', *ZTK* 60, 1963, p. 305, thinks that only a 'free' rhythm can be established in the prologue.

14. See p. 17 above.

15. See the article cited on p. 104, n. 17 above.

16. H. Leroy, 'Das johanneische Missverständnis als literarische Form', *Bibel und Leben* 9, 1968, pp. 196ff., believes that this is strongly conditioned by literary factors.

Chapter Five

1. M. Simon, *Les sectes juives au temps de Jésus*, 1961.

2. See also L. Goppelt, *Christentum und Judentum im 1. und 2. Jahrhundert*, 1954, pp. 131ff.; H. J. Schoeps, *Urgemeinde, Judenchristentum, Gnosis*, 1956, pp. 44ff.; W. D. Davies, *Christian Origins and Judaism*, 1962, pp. 19ff.; G. Kretschmar, 'Zur religionsgeschichtlichen Einordnung der Gnosis', *EvTh* 19, 1959, pp. 354ff.; W. C. van Unnik, 'Die jüdische Komponente in der

Enstehung der Gnosis', *VigChr* 15, 1961, pp. 65f.; M. Hengel, *Judaism and Hellenism* I, 1974, p. 243, speaks of Chaldaean-Essene 'gnosis' as an 'encyclopaedic wisdom'.

3. O. Cullmann, *Le problème littéraire et historique du roman pseudoclémentin. Etude sur le rapport entre le gnosticisme et le judéo-christianisme*, 1930.

4. F. M. Braun, *Jean le théologien*, Vol. II, 1964: id., 'S. Jean, la Sagesse et l'Histoire', *Neotestamentica et Patristica. Festschrift für Oscar Cullmann*, 1962, pp. 123ff.; A. Feuillet, *Etudes johanniques*, 1962.

5. A. Schlatter, commentary, ³1960. See also H. L. Strack–P. Billerbeck, *Kommentar zum NT aus Talmud und Midrasch*, Vol. II, pp. 302ff.

6. C. H. Dodd, *The Interpretation of the Fourth Gospel*, 1953: see also D. Daube, *The New Testament and Rabbinic Judaism*, 1956.

7. According to the theory of A. Guilding, *The Fourth Gospel and Jewish Worship*, 1960, the author kept to the sequence of narratives in the Jewish festal calendar.

8. H. Odeberg, *The Fourth Gospel in its Relation to the Contemporaneous Currents in Palestine and the Hellenistic-Oriental World*, reprinted 1929: see also G. Scholem, *Jüdische Mystik in ihren Hauptströmungen*, 1957.

9. See also G. Quispel, 'Jüdische Gnosis und jüdische Heterodoxie', *EvTh* 14, 1954, pp. 474ff. I do not quite understand why W. G. Kümmel, *Introduction to the New Testament*, revd edn 1975, on the one hand shows well how 'Gnostic religion arose in Syrian territory in the first century in connection with *some fringe developments in Judaism*' (my italics), while at the same time he draws such a sharp distinction between this 'Jewish gnosis' and 'heterodox Judaism', associating only the former and not the latter with the origin of the Gospel of John (p. 226). Is this a question of terminology? (See below, p. 35). S. Schulz, *Untersuchungen zur Menschensohn-Christologie im Johannesevangelium*, 1957, p. 116, rightly stresses that 'the boundaries between a heterodox Judaism and a gnosticizing Judaism are very fluid'.

10. S. Schulz, *Komposition und Herkunft der johanneischen Reden*, 1960, in a continuation of his *Untersuchungen zur Menschensohn-Christologie im Johannesevangelium*, 1957, indicates the various trends of this Judaism which appear in the Fourth Gospel.

11. But this has recently been questioned by E. Yamauchi, *Pre-Christian Gnosticism. A Survey of the Evidences*, 1973.

12. F. M. Braun, *Jean le Théologien*, Vol. II, 1964, whose fundamental investigation of the milieu and individual studies are to be recommended.

13. G. Baumbach, *Qumran und das Johannesevangelium*, 1957.

14. Herbert Braun, *Qumran und das Neue Testament*, 1966.

15. K. G. Kuhn, 'Johannesevangelium und Qumrantexte', *Neotestamentica et Patristica. Festschrift für O. Cullmann*, 1972, pp. 111ff.

16. See note 19 below.

17. J. Roloff, 'Der johanneische Lieblingsjünger und der Lehrer der Gerechtigkeit', *NTS* 16, 1969, pp. 129ff.; see below, p. 117, n. 25.

18. For the dualism of Qumran see W. Huppenbauer, *Der Mensch zwischen zwei Welten*, 1959. For its relationship with the Fourth Gospel see J. H. Charlesworth, 'A Critical Comparison of the Dualism in QS III, 13–IV, 26 and the "Dualism" contained in the Fourth Gospel', *NTS* 15, 1968/69, pp. 389ff.

19. O. Betz, *Der Paraklet, Fürsprecher im häretischen Spätjudentum, im Johannesevangelium und in neugefundenen gnostischen Schriften.* 1963.

20. O. Cullmann, *Pseudoclémentines*, and J. Thomas, *Le mouvement baptiste en Palestine et en Syrie*, 1935.

21. For the relationship with Qumran see now J. Schmitt, 'Le milieu baptiste de Jean le précurseur', *RSR* 47, 1973, pp. 391ff.

22. In addition to the next section see pp. 60, 66, 71f., 73, 79f., 90 below.

23. R. Bultmann, 'Die Bedeutung der neuerschlossenen mandäischen und manichäischen Quellen für das Verständnis des Johannesevangeliums', *ZNW* 24, 1925, pp. 100ff.

24. W. Baldensperger, *Der Prolog des 4. Evangeliums. Sein polemischer und apologetischer Zweck*, 1898.

25. K. Rudolph, *Die Mandäer*, I and II, 1960/61. This has recently been vigorously questioned by E. M. Yamauchi, *Pre-Christian Gnosticism* (p. 107, n. 11 above).

26. *Die Mandäer*, I, pp. 66ff.

27. See the very full critical survey by C. Colpe, *Die religionsgeschichtliche Schule. Darstellung und Kritik ihres Bildes vom gnostischen Erlösermythus*, 1961. Also in the commentary by R. Schnackenburg, Vol. I, p. 543, Excursus 6.

28. This is the tendency today. Is the sharp distinction made by W. G. Kümmel (sec n. 9 above) between Jewish gnosticism and heterodox Judaism also connected with this?

29. G. Bornkamm, 'Zur Interpretation des Johannesevangeliums', *Geschichte und Glaube, Gesammelte Aufsätze*, Vol. III, 1968, p. 118. Here he criticizes E. Käsemann's *The Testament of Jesus* not only for its charge of 'naive docetism' but also for its comments on the gnosticism of the Gospel. See pp. 119ff.; 'The gnostic features are not really understood in a gnostic way.' Here Bornkamm is nearer to Bultmann than to Käsemann. Like E. Ruckstuhl (see the article cited on p. 102, n. 12 above, p. 150), G. Bornkamm also refers to John 3.16, an anti-gnostic remark which Käsemann interprets in a different sense. For Käsemann's work see also H. Hegermann, 'Er kam in sein Eigentum. Zu der Bedeutung des Erdenwirkens Jesu im vierten Evangelium', *Festschrift für J. Jeremias*, 1970, pp. 112 ff.

30. See e.g. the article by Wayne A. Meeks, 'The Man from Heaven in Johannine Sectarianism', *JBL* 91, 1972, p. 44, which is also interesting in other respects. See p. 110, n. 1 below.

31. A. Feuillet, *Le Christ Sagesse de Dieu d'après les Epîtres pauliniennes*, 1966, and F. Christ, *Jesus Sophia. Die Sophia-Christologie bei den Synoptikern*, 1970.

32. See especially F. M. Braun, *Jean le Théologien*, Vol. II.

33. R. Harris–A. Mingana, *The Odes and Psalms of Solomon*, 1920; see also E. Hennecke–W. Schneemelcher-R. McL. Wilson, *New Testament Apocrypha* II, 1965, pp. 808–10. See too F. M. Braun, *Jean le Théologien*, I, pp. 232ff., and II, pp. 224ff.

34. Most recently H. Charlesworth, 'Les Odes de Salomon et les manuscrits de la mer morte', *RB* 77, 1970, pp. 522ff.

35. A. J. Festugière, *La Révélation d'Hermès Trismégiste* (4 vols), 1950/54. For an edition of the text see A. D. Nock–A. J. Festugière, *Corpus Hermeticum*, 1945/54.

36. See G. D. Kilpatrick, 'The Religious Background of the Fourth Gospel', in F. L. Cross (ed.), *Studies in the Fourth Gospel*, 1957, pp. 76ff.

37. In addition to my own work (see note 3 above) see the more recent investigation by G. Strecker, *Judenchristentum in den Pseudoklementinen*, 1958. Also see my 'Die neuentdeckten Qumrantexte und das Judenchristentum der Pseudoklementinen', *Festschrift für R. Bultmann*, 1954, pp. 35ff. (now also in O. Cullmann, *Vorträge und Aufsätze 1925–62*, pp. 241ff.).

38. Ed. by M. Malinine, H. C. Puech, G. Quispel, *Evangelium Veritatis*, 1956, 1961. See C. K. Barrett, 'The Theological Vocabulary of the Fourth Gospel and the Gospel of Truth', *Festschrift für O. Piper*, 1962, pp. 210ff.

39. For the whole discovery see J. M. Robinson, 'The Coptic Gnostic Library Today', *NTS* 14, 1967/68, pp. 356ff.

40. Ed. J. Macdonald, *Memar Marqah, The Teaching of Marqah*, BZAW 84 i and ii, 1963.

41. M. Gaster, *The Samaritans, Their History, Doctrines and Literature*, 1925.

42. J. Macdonald, *The Theology of the Samaritans*, 1964.

43. See the more recent bibliographies by L. A. Mayer and D. Broadribb, *Bibliography of the Samaritans*, 1964, and by P. Sacchi, 'Studi Samaritani', *Rivista di Storia e Letteratura religiose*, 1969, pp. 413ff. During the publication of the present work R. J. Coggins, *Samaritans and Jews*, 1974, appeared.

44. W. G. Kümmel, *Introduction*, [2]1975, p. 227, speaks summarily, in contrast to his otherwise cautious judgments, of the 'wholly unproved assertion that John was influenced by Samaritanism'.

45. O. Cullmann, 'Samaria and the Origins of the Christian Mission (1953/54)', in *The Early Church*, 1956, 185–92: id., 'L'opposition contre le temple de Jérusalem motif commun de la théologie johannique et du monde ambiant', *NTS* 5, 1958/59, pp. 157ff. (it also appears in expanded form in *Vorträge und Aufsätze 1920–1962*, pp. 260ff.).

46. Above all J. Bowman, 'Samaritan Studies', *BJRL* 41, 1958, pp. 298ff., and *Samaritanische Probleme, Studien zum Verhältnis von Samaritanertum, Judentum und Christentum*, 1967. Following him, E. D. Freed, 'Samaritan Influence in the Gospel of John', *CBQ* 30, 1968, pp. 580ff.: id., 'Did John write his Gospel partly to win Samaritan Converts?', *NT* 12, 1970, pp.

241ff.: C. H. H. Scobie, 'The Origins and Development of Samaritan Christianity', *NTS* 20, 1973, pp. 390ff. I have again discussed the problem in the light of more recent works in 'La Samarie et les origines Chrétiennes', *Mélanges d'histoire ancienne pour W. Seston*, 1974, pp. 135ff.

For the relationship of Samaria to gnosticism, especially to the Dositheans and the Sethians, see W. Beltz, 'Samaritanertum und Gnosis', in *Gnosis und Neues Testament*, ed. K. W. Tröger, 1973, pp. 89ff.

47. However, John 4.22 must then be seen as a qualification, as a recognition of the fact that the way of salvation leads via the Jews. G. W. Buchanan gives another explanation of the designation 'the Jews' in connection with Samaritan influence on John, see below, pp. 51f.

Chapter Six

1. As has already been mentioned, he speaks of an '*ecclesiola in ecclesia*' (see p. 15 above); W. A. Meeks (see the article cited on p. 108, n. 30 above) speaks of a 'sect'. Before them, A. Kragerud in particular postulated the existence of a Johannine group. Of course his collective interpretation of the 'beloved disciple' is very problematical. See A. Kragerud, *Der Lieblingsjünger im Johannesevangelium*, 1959.

2. Thus E. Käsemann, *The Testament of Jesus*, 1968, p. 39.

3. E. Lohmeyer, *Galilee and Jerusalem*, 1936.

4. It has already been suggested that on the contrary they should be called 'Hebrews' (see E. Trocmé, *Le livre des Actes et l'Histoire*, 1957, pp. 190f.). This discussion seems to me to be unimportant. Similarly C. H. H. Scobie, 'The Origins and Development of Samaritan Christianity', *NTS* 20, 1973, p. 399; 'This question must remain open.' In the further course of his article he speaks of the 'Stephen-Philip group'. In what follows I shall use the customary term and call the members of the group 'Hellenists'.

5. See Oscar Cullmann, *Vorträge und Aufsätze 1925–1962*, the section 'Sonderströmungen des Judentums und ältesten Christentums', pp. 225ff.; among the articles collected there see especially the German translation by K. Fröhlich of the article 'Le scoperte recenti e l'enigma del Vangelo di Giovanni', *Studi e materiali di Storia delle religioni* 34, 1958, pp. 3ff.

6. M. Simon, *St Stephen and the Hellenists in the Primitive Church*, 1958.

7. Against M. H. Scharlemann, *Stephen a Singular Saint* (Analecta Biblica 1968, see below, pp. 50f. and p. 113, nn. 42, 43). The *argumentum e silentio* is wrongly used by Scharlemann to question Stephen's membership of the Hellenist group. The contrary emerges so evidently from the context that Luke did not really need to say explicitly that Stephen was one of the Hellenists. R. Scroggs, 'The Earliest Hellenistic Christianity', in *Religions in Antiquity, Festschrift for E. R. Goodenough*, 1968, pp. 176ff., and L. Gaston,

No Stone on Another, 1970, pp. 154ff., regard Stephen as a member of the group.

8. It is significant that despite his tendency to make light of the differences existing within the primitive community, Luke allowed this important note to stand; E. Haenchen, *The Acts of the Apostles*, 1971, ad loc., wrongly attributes it to Luke himself.

9. It has been asserted that this note, too, should be attributed to Luke. But could one not say that it, too, is in contrast to his tendency to keep quiet about tensions or to play down their significance?

10. Thus rightly, among others, L. Gaston, op. cit., pp. 154ff., who also stresses the affinity with the Samaritans. The report of the martyrdom of Stephen which provides a framework might also come from a source or a special tradition from Stephen's circle, or from converted Samaritans.

11. See B. Reicke, *Glaube und Leben der Urgemeinde*, 1957, pp. 129ff.

12. See A. M. Goldberg, *Untersuchungen über die Vorstellung von der Schekinah in der frühen rabbinischen Literatur*, 1969.

13. R. Reitzenstein–H. H. Schäder, *Studien zum antiken Synkretismus aus Iran und Griechenland*, 1926, p. 318.

14. It is interesting, in connection with the theory I develop here, that among the Samaritans Bethel is identified with Gerizim. See J. Bowman, 'The Samaritans and the Book of Deuteronomy', *Glasgow Oriental Society*, 1957/58, pp. 13f.

15. During the printing of the present book an interesting work has appeared by W. D. Davies, *The Gospel and the Land*, 1974. I note that in the chapter on the Fourth Gospel (pp. 288ff.) he puts forward a theory which I stated as early as 1958 (see my article cited on p. 109, n. 45 above) and have repeated often since, that places of worship have been replaced by the person of Christ. (Among other instances, he gives the very ones which I mention above and had already given in my 1958/59 article, pp. 70f.) He ascribes the discovery of the connection between the Gospel of John and the Hellenists (and the Samaritans), on p. 294, n. 10, to R. E. Brown and quotes his commentary, which appeared in 1966, p. 122. However, at this point Brown refers explicitly to my 1958/59 article.

16. See O. Cullmann, *Early Christian Worship*, 1953.

17. Unlike Qumran, where the stress on baptismal rites and common meals is governed by the rejection of the existing temple worship.

18. See pp. 95ff. below.

19. See T. F. Glasson, *Moses in the Fourth Gospel*, SBT 40, 1963. Now also W. A. Meeks, *The Prophet-King. Moses Traditions and the Johannine Christology*, 1967, and C. H. H. Scobie, 'Origins and Development' (n. 4 above), p. 406.

20. See S. Schulz, *Menschensohn-Christologie* (p. 107, n. 9 above), who stresses the reinterpretation of the apocalyptic conception of the Son of Man in terms of Hellenistic and Gnostic views. E. Kinniburgh, 'The Johannine Son of Man', *Studia Evangelica* 4, 1968, pp. 64ff., also stresses

the abandonment of its apocalyptic character. See also O. Cullmann. *The Christology of the New Testament*, ²1963, pp. 181ff., and C. Colpe, υἱὸς τοῦ ἀνθρώπου, *TDNT* 8, pp. 468ff.: also Excursus 5 in R. Schnackenburg, commentary, pp. 529ff.

21. G. Bornkamm, 'Der Paraklet im Johannesevangelium', *Festschrift für R. Bultmann*, 1949, pp. 12ff. Also T. Preiss, *Le Fils de l'Homme*, 1951, p. 23: see below, p. 118, n. 7. For the intercession of Moses see the next section. U. B. Müller, 'Die Parakletenvorstellung im Johannesevangelium', *ZTK* 71, 1974, pp. 31ff., thinks that the connection between Son of Man and Paraclete in the Fourth Gospel should be challenged (pp. 37f.).

22. See the good survey of scholarship by P. de Robert, 'Les Samaritains et le Nouveau Testament', *Etudes Théologiques et Religieuses* 45, 1970, pp. 179ff.

23. See p. 16 above.

24. J. Bowman, 'Samaritan Studies' (see p. 109, n. 46 above), pp. 301f.

25. Luke also shows his interest in Samaria in his Gospel, in his account of the life of Jesus. See P. de Robert, op. cit., p. 182. Luke evidently had special traditions for the Gospel as well as for Acts, which came either from the Hellenist groups or from converted Samaritans.

26. F. M. Braun has drawn my attention to an interesting *literary* parallel between John 4 and Acts 8 (though in connection with the intervention of Peter and John); the expression ἡ δωρεὰ τοῦ θεοῦ *only* occurs in the two passages John 4.10 and Acts 8.20.

27. For the question of the authenticity of the logion see p. 90 below.

28. O. Cullmann, 'Samaria and the Origins of the Christian Mission', *The Early Church*, 1956, pp. 185–92.

29. Despite the fact that there is a connection between John the Baptist and his disciples and Samaria (see p. 115, n. 11 below), the identification of the *alloi* with the Hellenists on the basis of the evidence in Acts 8 seems to me more likely than the identification with John the Baptist and his followers proposed by J. A. T. Robinson, *Twelve New Testament Studies*, SBT 34, 1962, pp. 61ff. Nevertheless J. A. T. Robinson has pointed out in this article a connection of the disciples of the Baptist, the Hellenists and the Johannine circle with Samaria which is important for my theory.

30. The general attitude to Peter (see pp. 55, 72, 74f., 78) fits with this. I do not see why W. G. Kümmel, *Introduction*, p. 220, thinks that my argument about the *alloi* can be refuted by pointing out that the opposition to the Jerusalem temple in John is quite different in character from that in Qumran. I do not dispute that point (see n. 52 below and pp. 53, 91). In the identification of the *alloi* I am not so much concerned with the connection between the Hellenists and Qumran as with the connection between the Hellenists and the Gospel of John. I would also stress this over against C. H. H. Scobie, op. cit., p. 408 (see also p. 114, n. 52), with whom I otherwise largely agree.

31. *Alloi* could be the word used by the evangelist to describe those

standing particularly close to him. See what is said on p. 73, p. 117, n. 18 below about the *allos mathetes*.

32. A. F. J. Klijn, 'Stephen's Speech, Acts VII, 2–53', *NTS* 4, 1957, pp. 25ff. See also P. Geoltrain, 'Esséniens et Hellénistes', *TZ* 15, 1959, pp. 241ff.

33. See op. cit., pp. 94, 113ff. I do not, however, believe that this affinity is to be explained by the influence of the Hellenists on gnostic Jewish Christianity: both Hellenists and Ebionites will go back to heterodox Judaism.

34. E. A. Plumptre, 'The Samaritan Element in the Gospels and Acts', *The Expositor* 10, 1878, pp. 22ff.

35. Anchor Bible 1967.

36. Abram Spiro, 'Stephen's Samaritan Background', pp. 285ff.

37. This was already established by P. Kahle, 'Untersuchungen zur Geschichte des Pentateuchtextes', *Theologische Studien und Kritike* 1915, pp. 399ff.

38. See above, p. 109, n. 46.

39. See op. cit., p. 110, n. 7.

40. According to the Samaritans, Gerizim is related to the tabernacle, see J. Macdonald, *The Theology of the Samaritans*, p. 445.

41. Other factors are the considerable role of Moses and the special traditions about him, like his eloquence (Acts 7.22). P. Benoit, *RB* 72, 1965, p. 619, considers the possibility that the latter feature, like other details of the speech which differ from our Old Testament, is Samaritan (against J. Bihler, who regards Stephen's speech as Lukan).

42. Unfortunately the thorough comparison of the speech and Samaritan sources in Scharlemann's dissertation is associated with some very dubious assertions about Stephen's complete independence and isolation from the rest of primitive Christianity.

43. See my remarks about Scharlemann's work in my article, 'La Samarie et les origines chrétiennes', *Mélanges d'Histoire ancienne pour W. Seston*, 1974, pp. 135ff.; see also the criticism by F. F. Bruce in *JBL* 88, 1969, p. 114.

44. See p. 110, n. 7 above.

45. J. Bowman, 'Samaritan Studies I. The Fourth Gospel and the Samaritans', *BJRL* 41, 1958, pp. 298ff., and id., *Samaritanische Probleme. Studien zum Verhältnis von Samaritanertum, Judentum und Christentum*, 1967.

46. W. A. Meeks, *The Prophet-King* (above, p. 111, n. 19).

47. Ibid., p. 316.

48. G. W. Buchanan, 'The Samaritan Origin of the Gospel of John', *Religions in Antiquity, Festschrift for E. R. Goodenough*, 1968, pp. 149ff.

49. See my conjecture (p. 38 above) that *Ioudaioi* is a more general designation for official Judaism in contrast to heterodox Judaism.

50. See O. Cullmann, 'La Samarie et les origines chrétiennes', *Mélanges Seston*, 1974, pp. 135ff.

51. The otherwise excellent article by C. H. H. Scobie (p. 110, n. 46 above) overlooks the importance in this triangular relationship of the rejection of any liturgical link with a place of worship, *common to both Stephen's speech and the Gospel of John*. This seems to me fundamental to the whole question.

52. C. H. H. Scobie charges me (op. cit., p. 399) with having overlooked the difference between Hellenists and Qumran in their rejection of the temple, but this is certainly unjustified. See my earlier articles collected in the chapter 'Sonderströmungen des Judentums und altesten Christentums', *Vorträge und Aufsätze 1925–1962*, e.g. pp. 281ff.

53. Thus e.g. H. Conzelmann, 'Was von Anfang war', *Festschrift für R. Bultmann*, 1954, pp. 194ff. W. Thüsing, 'Glaube an die Liebe. Die Johannesbriefe', in *Gestalt und Anspruch des Neuen Testaments*, 1969, pp. 282ff., thinks of a group of disciples very closely connected with the eye-witnesses.

54. However, despite the fundamental difference, the eschatological view of Revelation does not exclude the present (see M. Rissi, *Was ist und was danach geschehen soll. Die Zeit- und Geschichtsauffassung der Offenbarung des Johannes*, ²1965), while the perspective of the Gospel does not exclude the future (see P. Ricca, *Die Eschatologie des 4. Evangeliums*, 1966).

55. But the terminology is different: *arnion—amnos*.

56. For Revelation and liturgy see O. Cullmann, *Early Christian Worship*, 1953, pp. 7, 21; G. Delling, 'Zum gottesdienstlichen Stil der Johannes-Apokalypse', *NT* 1, 1959, pp. 107ff.; T. F. Torrance, 'Liturgie et Apocalypse', *Verbum Caro* 11, 1957, pp. 28 ff.; S. Läuchli, 'Eine Gottesdienststruktur in der Johannesoffenbarung', *TZ* 16, 1960, pp. 359 ff.; A. Feuillet, *L'Apocalypse*, 1963, p. 71; P. Prigent, *Apocalypse et Liturgie*, 1964: E. Lohse, commentary, NTD 1971.

57. However, we also find traces in Revelation of another tradition which, like that of Judaism, knows of a heavenly temple (Rev. 11.19).

58. J. N. Sanders makes an interesting connection in 'St John on Patmos', *NTS* 9, 1962/63, pp. 75ff., by identifying the author of Revelation with the author of the Gospel (whom he believes to be John Mark).

59. According to P. Kahle, 'Untersuchungen' (n. 36 above), pp. 410f., Heb. 9.3 presupposes the use of the Samaritan Pentateuch. Heb. 9.11 should be compared with Acts 7.48.

60. W. Manson, *The Epistle to the Hebrews*, 1951. Before him see already E. F. Scott, *The Epistle to the Hebrews. Its Doctrine and Significance*, 1923, pp. 62ff.

61. C. Spicq, *L'Epître aux Hébreux* (2 vols), 1952, 1953.

62. Y. Yadin, *The Dead Sea Scrolls and the Epistle to the Hebrews*, 1958: H. Kosmala, *Hebräer-Essener-Christen*, 1959.

63. E. A. Knox, 'The Samaritans and the Epistle to the Hebrews', *The Churchman* 22, 1927, pp. 184ff. I owe this reference to C. H. H. Scobie, op. cit., p. 409.

64. On this see the interesting remarks by C. H. H. Scobie, op. cit., pp. 409ff.

65. For the relationship between Peter and the beloved disciple see below, pp. 72, 74, 78 and S. Agourides, 'Peter and John in the Fourth Gospel', *Studia Evangelica* 4, 1968, pp. 3ff. J. Schmitt, 'Le groupe johannique et la chrétienté apostolique', *Colloque du Cerdic*, Strasbourg 1971, pp. 169ff., puts strong stress on this connection.

66. See above, pp. 41f.

67. See above, p. 42.

Chapter Seven

1. See above, pp. 7, 24.

2. See above, pp. 46, 49.

3. In this form I can agree with the theory of the more recent works, see above p. 46. But see p. 59.

4. See below, p. 00.

5. Against G. Bornkamm and E. Ruckstuhl, see above, p. 108 n. 29.

6. Among others, K. H. Schelkle, *Das Neue Testament. Seine literarische und theologische Geschichte*, 1966, p. 95, assumes anti-gnostic polemic.

7. I am not speaking here of the influence of *converted* representatives of heterodox and above all of Samaritan Judaism (considered above, pp. 46f., 49).

8. See above, p. 109, n. 37.

9. See F. M. Braun, *OrLov* 11, 1967, p. 229.

10. See my book on the Pseudo-Clementines cited on p. 107, n. 3 above, though as a result of the researches of K. Rudolph, *Die Mandäer*, I, 1960, pp. 66ff., I no longer assume any direct connection with the Mandaeans.

11. See C. H. H. Scobie, *John the Baptist*, 1964, pp. 163ff.: also the work by J. A. T. Robinson cited on p. 112, n. 29.

12. W. Baldensperger, *Der Prolog des 4. Evangeliums* (p. 108, n. 24).

13. W. Bauer, 'Der religionsgeschichtliche Hintergrund des Prologs zum Johannesevangelium', *Eucharisterion II für H. Gunkel*, 1923, pp. 3ff. See also his commentary.

14. See his commentary.

15. Thus too H. Thyen, 'Βάπτισμα μετανοίας εἰς ἄφεσιν ἁμαρτιῶν', *Zeit und Geschichte, Festschrift für R. Bultmann*, 1964, pp. 117ff. Without following this theory, R. E. Brown, commentary, p. 28, is inclined to follow H. Thyen, op. cit., in assuming that the Baptist sect already celebrated John the Baptist as 'the light' on the basis of Zechariah's hymn in Luke 1.68ff., which prophesies that the child John will be a light for those who are 'in darkness'.

16. For the cult of Simon see L. Cerfaux, 'La gnose simonienne', *Gesammelte Aufsätze* I, 1954, pp. 191ff. While this book was being printed, K. Beyschlag, *Simon Magus und die christliche Gnosis*, 1974, appeared,

arguing that Simonianism only arose in the second century and so was not a prelude to Christian gnosticism.

17. Thus too R. Schnackenburg, commentary, p. 268, and R. E. Brown, commentary, p. 31. Also G. Bornkamm, op. cit., p. 117. For this question see now E. Schweizer, 'Jesus der Zeuge Gottes. Zum Problem des Doketismus im Johannesevangelium', *Festschrift für J. N. Sevenster*, 1970, pp. 161ff.

18. The Jewish Christians of the Pseudo-Clementines also display docetic tendencies.

Chapter Eight

1. F. M. Braun, *Jean le Théologien* (p. 102, n. 3), Vol. I.

2. Put forward in rather a different form e.g. by A. Harnack.

3. See above, pp. 9f.

4. This would be most likely on the assumption of F. M. Braun's hypothesis that the writer of the Gospel was simply a secretary.

5. See above, pp. 17ff.

6. The question whether this also implies that the whole Johannine circle comes from Judaea must remain open. The tendency of scholars concerned with the Samaritan question is to put the circle in the north and even to describe the Gospel as 'northern' (see J. Bowman, *Samaritanische Probleme*, p. 56). This seems to me to be doubtful, despite the strong interest of the Gospel in Samaria.

7. Eusebius, *HE* V, 20, 4.

8. E. Schwartz, *Über den Tod der Söhne Zebedaei*, 1904. Already put forward before him by A. Réville, *Jésus de Nazareth*, I, 1897, pp. 354f. The argument that the saying would not have been handed down unless the two sons had been martyred would only be valid if we knew the stages in its transmission. On the contrary, one might assume that Mark 10.39a provided the stimulus for the late account of the simultaneous death of the two brothers.

9. The demand of the sons of Zebedee in Luke 9.51 for fire to be brought down on a Samaritan city is hardly reconcilable with the special interest of the author of the Gospel of John in Samaria.

10. See above, p. 64.

11. A. Harnack, *Die Chronologie der altchristlichen Literatur bis Eusebius*, 1897, pp. 659ff.

12. J. Colson, *L'énigme du disciple que Jésus aimait*, 1969, assumes a confusion between this John and the son of Zebedee.

13. The variant which puts the article before *allos* is almost certainly secondary.

14. See R. E. Brown, commentary, p. xciv. In this case the article before *allos* in 20.2 has also been added by the redactor.

15. This *a priori* underlies the arguments of R. E. Brown and R. Schnackenburg.

16. Even in Mark, the saying of Jesus which designates the betrayer, 'it is one of the Twelve' (Mark 14.20), seems to presuppose, despite Mark 14.17, that others were present in addition to the Twelve.

17. R. Schnackenburg, commentary, p. 77, also expresses doubt here.

18. See above, p. 73. Is it too bold to recall here also the *alloi* of 4.38 whom we have identified with the Hellenists (see above, p. 49)? Might not *allos* or *alloi* be a designation behind which the author, or those who are particularly close to him, take refuge?

19. See pp. 69f. above: Galilean education (Acts 4.13), a different Jewish circle, nickname 'sons of thunder'.

20. Johannes Weiss, *Earliest Christianity* II, 1937 (reprinted 1959), p. 788, and P. Parker, 'John and John Mark', *JBL* 79, 1960, pp. 97ff. See also J. E. Bruns, 'John Mark; A Riddle within the Johannine Enigma', *Scripture* 18, 1963, pp. 88f.; L. Johnson, 'Who was the Beloved Disciple?', *ExpT* 77, 1966, pp. 157ff. (and the discussion by J. R. Porter, ibid., p. 213).

21. P. Parker, op. cit., moreover refers to the fact that the identification with John Mark would also explain the influence of the Gospels of Luke and Mark on John, though this influence is questionable (see above, pp. 5f.).

22. As early as the year 1900, J. Kreyenbühl, *Das Evangelium der Wahrheit*, pp. 157ff., suggested that the beloved disciple, Lazarus and the author (who in his view was writing at the time of Hadrian) were identical. In line with his general approach, however, he thinks in terms of mystic communion with Christ. More recently, and quite independently of Kreyenbühl's otherwise somewhat arbitrary construction, see F. V. Filson, 'Who was the Beloved Disciple?', *JBL* 68, 1949, pp. 83ff.; K. A. Eckhardt, *Der Tod des Johannes*, 1961. See also J. N. Sanders, 'Those whom Jesus Loved', *NTS* 1, 1954/55, pp. 29ff. However, according to him the author of the Gospel is John Mark, who is supposed to have preserved the memoirs of Lazarus.

23. It is interesting that Rudolf Steiner, the founder of anthroposophy, also ascribes the Gospel to Lazarus, though without support from historical considerations.

24. In the probably unnecessary search for a name, even Matthias, the replacement apostle of Acts 1.23ff., has been mentioned (see E. L. Titus, 'The Identity of the Beloved Disciple', *JBL* 69, 1950, pp. 323ff.). He has already had to fill a whole series of lacunae in antiquity.

25. J. Roloff, 'Der johanneische Lieblingsjünger und der Lehrer der Gerechtigkeit' (above, p. 107, n. 17), compares the 'beloved disciple' with the 'Teacher of Righteousness' at Qumran.

26. See above, pp. 66ff.

27. See above, pp. 72f.

28. See above, p. 57.

29. G. Hoffmann, *Das Johannesevangelium als Alterswerk*, 1933. However, he thinks that the style should be characterized as 'elderly'; this could be

problematical. (See also the criticism by R. Schnackenburg, commentary, p. 92.)

30. See above, pp. 5ff., 24.

31. See above, pp. 12ff., 20ff.

32. See below, p. 89.

33. Albert Schweitzer, *Geschichte der Leben-Jesu-Forschung*, [2]1913, p. 310 (this passage does not appear in the English translation).

34. Also those mentioned in the Pseudo-Clementines.

35. Matt. 11.25: Luke 10.21, where the scribes are in view, does not tell against this. In Matt. 10.27b, a passage which has been mentioned earlier, the disciples have 'whispered in their ear' what they are to proclaim on the rooftops.

36. See above, p. 64 and the following pages below.

37. See above, p. 69.

Chapter Nine

1. See above, pp. 15, 110, n. 1.

2. O. Cullmann, *Early Christian Worship*, 1953.

3. However, even in heterodox Judaism this very varied opposition to the existing temple in Jerusalem had led to washings and common meals acquiring ritual significance, see above, p. 111, n. 17.

4. See above, p. 39.

5. For this question see also my 'Von Jesus zur Stephanusgruppe und zum Johannesevangelium', in *Jesus und Paulus, Festschrift für W. G. Kummel*, 1975.

6. O. Cullmann, *The Christology of the New Testament*, [2]1963, pp. 137ff. H. E. Tödt, *The Son of Man in the Synoptic Tradition*, 1965, follows Bultmann in putting forward the opposite view.

7. See R. Otto, *The Kingdom of God and the Son of Man*, 1938: also E. Sjöberg, *Der Menschensohn im äthiopischen Henochbuch*, 1946, p. 115. For the question of the Son of Man in John see also the works cited on p. 111, n. 20 above. T. Preiss, *Le fils de l'homme*, 1951, shows that the intercessory Son of Man (see above p. 45 on the relationship between the Son of Man and the Paraclete, and the intercessions of Moses) also goes back to Jesus. He refers to Matt. 25.31ff.: Mark 8.38.

8. Not only opposition to the *present* temple, as in the Qumran sect, who envisage that after their victory a temple will be built which will stand until finally God himself builds his own temple. See the most recently discovered temple scroll about which Y. Yadin, 'The Temple Scroll', *BA* 30, 1967, pp. 135ff. gives a preliminary report. He is preparing an edition.

9. A. Jaubert, *La date de la Cène. Calendrier biblique et Liturgie chrétienne*, 1957; ead., 'Jésus et le Calendrier de Qumran', *NTS* 7, 1960/61, 1ff. (but see J. Blinzler, 'Qumrankalender und Passionschronologie', *ZNW* 49, 1958, 238ff.).

10. See the interpretation I give in my article "Ο ὀπίσω μου ἐρχόμενος᾽, *The Early Church*, 1956, 177–82, following F. Dibelius, 'Zwei Worte Jesu', *ZNW* 9, 1910, pp. 190ff.

11. F. Hahn, *Mission in the New Testament*, SBT 47, 1965, pp. 54f., ascribes it to the 'school' of Matthew ('the particularistic Judaism of Palestine'). On the other hand J. Jeremias, *Jesus' Promise to the Nations*, SBT 24, [2]1967, 20ff., argues for the authenticity of the saying (reference to Matt. 10.23).

12. See above, pp. 48f.

13. To explain these stories as arising from Luke's well-known universalism (thus M. S. Enslin, 'Luke and the Samaritans', *HTR* 36, 1943, pp. 277f.) does not seem to me to be justified by their content. It is certainly in line with Luke's tendency to include these elements of tradition, which probably derive from Hellenist groups or converted Samaritans, in his Gospel, but they do not have the character of secondary 'compositions'. Luke's interest in Samaria is also clear from Acts.

14. See above, p. 114, n. 52.

15. For the whole question of Jesus and the temple see also my 'Von Jesus zu Stephanus und zum Johannesevangelium' (p. 118, n. 5 above).

16. See S. Schulz, *Untersuchungen zur Menschensohn-Christologie im Johannesevangelium*, 1959, and O. Cullmann, *Christology of the New Testament*, pp. 181ff. (see above, pp. 45, 89).

17. See the thorough investigation by F. Christ, *Jesus Sophia* (p. 108, n. 31 above).

18. G. Klein, *Die zwölf Apostel*, 1961.

19. E. H. Plumptre, 'The Samaritan Element in the Gospels and Acts', *The Expositor* 10, 1878, pp. 22f. (see p. 113, n. 34 above), even introduces the hypothesis that Stephen and Philip belonged to the seventy.

20. See pp. 81f. above.

21. This is not to be regarded as community tradition, despite W. Wrede, *The Messianic Secret* (1901), 1971. See O. Cullmann, *The Christology of the New Testament*, [2]1963, p. 124, and id., *The State in the New Testament*, 1957.

22. See above, p. 106, n. 9.

Chapter Ten

1. See above, pp. 67f., 79, and below, p. 97.

2. A. Loisy, *Le quatrième évangile*, 1921.

3. C. Maurer, *Ignatius von Antiochien und das Johannesevangelium*, 1949. H. Köster, 'Geschichte und Kultur im Johannesevangelium und bei Ignatius', *ZTK* 54, 1957, pp. 56ff., puts forward the opposite view. The question, however, is whether Ignatius is not one of the later representatives of an offshoot of the Johannine circle (at an advanced stage). See above, p. 61, and below, p. 98.

4. M.-E. Boismard, 'Clément de Rome et l'évangile de Jean', *RB* 55, 1948, pp. 376ff.

5. See G. Quispel, 'L'évangile de Jean et la Gnose', *Recherches bibliques de Louvain*, 1958, pp. 197ff.

6. See G. Mayeda, *Das Leben Jesu Fragment Egerton 2*, 1946.

7. At all events this is an important element in the theory advanced by W. Wilkens, *Die Entstehungsgeschichte* (above p. 102, n. 5).

8. R. M. Grant, 'The Origin of the Fourth Gospel', *JBL* 70, 1950, p. 305, also assumes an early date: see more recently F. L. Cribbs, 'A Reassessment of the Date and the Destination of the Gospel of John', *JBL* 90, 1970, pp. 38ff.

9. At any event, it is not a result of conservative principles!

10. E. R. Goodenough, 'John a Primitive Gospel', *JBL* 65, 1945, pp. 145ff., gives reasons which cause him to date the Gospel earlier. F. Spitta (p. 102 above) even goes back before AD 44 for his *Grundschrift*.

11. See p. 119, n. 3 above.

12. See p. 119, n. 3.

13. See the article cited on p. 109, n. 37 above.

14. See p. 60 above. H. E. Edwards, *The Disciple who wrote These Things*, 1953, also transfers the origin of the Fourth Gospel to Transjordania.

15. See above, pp. 53f.

16. Thus F. M. Braun, *Jean le Théologien*, Vol. I.

INDEX OF MODERN AUTHORS

INDEX OF BIBLICAL REFERENCES